I've travelled the world twice over,
Met the famous: saints and sinners,
Poets and artists, kings and queens,
Old stars and hopeful beginners,
I've been where no-one's been before,
Learned secrets from writers and cooks
All with one library ticket
To the wonderful world of books.

ANYTHING BUT HOUSEWORK

With an amusingly light touch, Jean Goodman describes her career as a journalist and radio/television personality and its effect upon her own private life. She tells of her various jobs on newspapers and magazines and some memorable interviews on other media. She also writes about her childhood in Leeds and her subsequent move to East Anglia, the alterations and additions to the family house, her visitor's book, her endearing but self-willed beagle and her own individualistic style of the culinary arts.

JEAN GOODMAN

ANYTHING BUT HOUSEWORK

Complete and Unabridged

ULVERSCROFT
Leicester

JUN 07 1994

First published in Great Britain

First Large Print Edition
published October 1993

British Library CIP Data

Goodman, Jean
Anything but housework.—Large print ed.—
Ulverscroft large print series: non-fiction
I. Title
070.92

ISBN 0–7089–2956–7

Published by
F. A. Thorpe (Publishing) Ltd.
Anstey, Leicestershire
Set by Words & Graphics Ltd.
Anstey, Leicestershire
Printed and bound in Great Britain by
T. J. Press (Padstow) Ltd., Padstow, Cornwall

This book is printed on acid-free paper

To my husband who, for obvious
reasons, prefers to remain
anonymous

"If you cannot work with love, but only with distaste, it is better that you should leave your work and sit at the gate of the temple and take alms of those who work with joy,"

Kahil Gibran

1

Beginnings

1

Beginnings

IT was "Children's Day" in the City of Leeds where I was born. All morning, the gaily-decorated floats had driven in procession along the main streets from the Town Hall to the public park, three miles out, in the suburbs. Each float carried a tableau of fancy-dressed children representing an historic episode in the life of the town. There were the Ancient Britons in skins, grimacing fiendishly as they brandished their clubs and axes, their faces and limbs streaked with woad; young archers pretended to fire make-believe arrows into the crowd; the local wool trade was portrayed by a little girl at a spinning wheel and a boy sitting at his loom, surrounded by carefully-draped sheepskins; there were sooty coal miners and neatly-uniformed cadets, representing the Red Cross and the Fire Brigade; Boy Scouts endlessly laying their camp fire and even a maypole with dancers managing to give quite a creditable, if hardly spirited performance on their moving platform. Last of all, to the accompaniment of special cheers from the crowd, came the Queen of Children's Day, smiling self-consciously on her flower-bedecked throne, accompanied by her Maids of Honour who tossed posies from their baskets into the crowd.

I was one of the crowd. But I longed, with all my heart, to be dressed up and ride through the streets on a float, bowing and waving to the cheering people. But at seven years old, I was ineligible to take part, simply because I did not go to one of the large, red brick, council schools where the boys and girls on the floats were educated and where they whipped their tops and roller-skated and played boisterous games of 'tig' and hop-scotch, in the great concrete play-grounds, behind the iron railings. Every day I passed one of these schools and peered enviously through the railings on my way to and from the very exclusive private establishment where I was, supposedly,

2

being instructed in the first important steps in my pre-ordained career, in other words, I was "learning to be a lady."

We too played games of a sort, in the neat strip of garden that passed for a playground, behind the large, terrace house where 'school' consisted of two classrooms on the ground floor. They were restricted games: there was no concrete on which to draw chalk lines for hop-scotch or whip our tops or roller skate and not much room for 'tig'. Indeed, the best thing about playtime was the preliminary ritual for choosing sides or selecting a "he" for games which, to all intents and purposes, never really materialised. If ever there were a case of anticipation being better than realisation, this was it.

We would stand in a large circle, chanting the magic formula:

"One potato, two potato, three potato, four.
Five potato, six potato, seven potato, more."

3

The word "potato" was accompanied, every time, by a bump on our clenched fists, by the teller who stood in the middle of the circle. We held our grimy fists firmly in front of us until "more" coincided with a bump on one of them, whereupon we put it, with some hesitation, behind our back: two bumped fists meant we were 'out'; and so it went on, until there was just one outstretched fist left, belonging to the winner. But by the time this had happened and the game had got underway, as likely as not, the teacher would ring her handbell to signify "break" was over.

It was a significant incident, for nothing about my school came up to my expectations and I felt a sense of injustice that even spilled over into this public holiday. My father had taken me to see the procession and my mother had stayed at home to do the cooking and housework. As the Queen and her attendants drove past, he lifted me high on his shoulders, to get a better view. Rather reluctantly, I waved back to them, steadying myself with one hand on my father's rough, curly hair.

Their float was the last in the procession. After it disappeared, the crowds on the pavement dispersed and my father and I waited for one of the blue and yellow trams to start running again, clanging up the tracks in the middle of the road, along the route to the Park. When one arrived, we climbed up the steep open stairway onto the top, where I loved to ride. But, for once, I scarcely noticed the exciting, unfamiliar view of roadside gardens and back yards: I was too pre-occupied, trying to pretend that I was, in fact, part of the procession, riding not on a tram, but on one of the floats that must, by this time, have already arrived at the Park.

When we eventually arrived, the crowds were enormous and there were long queues at the gates, waiting for admission. I was afraid that, by the time we reached the turnstile and paid our entrance money, we should be too late to see the judging in the competition for the best decorated float. And then my father produced what, looking back, can best be described as his 'trump card': Holding me firmly by the hand, he strode up to a man guarding one of the side gates, pulled out his wallet and extracted a small, white visiting card. The gate-keeper scrutinised it, bowed slightly, handed the card back to my father, opened the gate and waved us through. And we had not even paid our admission money!

"How have we got in without paying?" I asked. My father took out his visiting card again and ran his thumb along the tiny printing on the right-hand bottom corner. It indicated he was the "local correspondent" for a national weekly magazine.

"What does it mean?" I asked.

He told me.

"But will you really write a story about this afternoon?" I asked.

"I might," he said.

"But if you don't?"

"It doesn't matter."

But it mattered to me! Suddenly and clearly I could visualise my mother in her apron, standing in the kitchen at home, bending over the sink or attending to something at the gas stove, while my jovial father had only to wave a little card with his name on it and the Park

6

gates opened miraculously before him. And this card, he had explained to me, represented not his real job, but just a part-time hobby. So there was injustice, it seemed, even out of school!

Suddenly, I no longer envied the council-school children, riding their decorated floats. I had almost forgotten about them for there was something far more exciting to think about: there and then, I decided that woman's work was not for me. One day, come what may, I too would be a journalist.

Journalism, as a career for women, was quite unacceptable in those days, but our family doctor, Dr Julius Friend, with unerring instinct, had almost decided that I should be a writer and that, in the fullness of time, I should have a little encouragement. He was the sort of general practitioner who not only treated his patient's physical ailments, but considered it was part of his responsibility to advise them on the, often far deeper, complications of their everyday lives. This was particularly so in the case of patients such as myself, who he had helped into the world and for whom he felt an additional responsibility.

Our family accepted his advice unquestionably and acknowledged his importance in our lives. It was an unwritten law that whenever his little blue two-seater car, with its jaunty back-seat dicky, was expected, the whisky decanter and one of the best cut-glass tumblers was waiting conveniently for him, on the hall table, where he deposited his rakish grey Hombourg and pale suede gloves, before going upstairs to see the patient. On his descent, if he felt so inclined, the "little refreshment" would accompany him into the sitting-room.

I loved his visits: not only did he invariably cure my sickness but he doctored my soul. My mother would usher him into the bedroom, fussily outline my symptoms and explain her own reasons for their cause. He would listen attentively, glaring at me from under his bushy eyebrows.

"Very interesting," he would ruminate, fingering his light-coloured, bushy moustache. "But now," and the eyebrows bristled imperiously, "suppose you just run along and leave the patient to me, to hear what SHE has to say. ALONE, if you please . . . " and, with a conspiratorial wink at me, he would dismiss my mother from the room. That alone, was quite an achievement, for a start!

On such an occasion, when I was about twelve years old, he sat on the side of my bed and took my pulse. He never bothered to use a thermometer. He sounded my chest with his stethoscope, folded it up and contemplated me speculatively. I lay back on the pillows, with drooping eyelids.

"Why," he asked, "don't you want to go to school?"

"It's so boring," I said, " . . . all this talk about it being the 'happiest days of your life.' That's rubbish."

"That depends," he said, "but you can have a couple of days off and I'll talk to your mother. But I think you could do worse than spend the time getting to know this gentleman:" from his attaché case he produced a small, red volume of Browning's poems.

Quite soon afterwards, I was told that I was to be sent away to boarding school. Before I went, I called at the Doctor's house to say "Goodbye". He had a small parcel waiting for me, a slim volume of poetry called *1914 and Other Poems*, by someone I had never heard of called Rupert Brooke. On the fly-leaf, in his meticulous flowing script, he had written:

"With Dr Friend's love, and hope that you will, one day, occupy a prominent place amongst the writers of verse."

"Not a poet. I can't write poetry. I'm going to be a journalist," I protested, trying out my ambition on someone for the very first time.

"Good enough," he responded: "just as long as you've decided to be a writer; any kind of writer; just stick to that." He was more than fifty years my senior and I was, of course, not a little in love with him. It passed, like the measles, but ever afterwards I remained passionately fond of Rupert Brooke's poems and rather susceptible to most doctors.

The large and rather select girls' boarding school in the Malvern Hills turned out to be, on the whole, a stimulating experience, apart from the weekly embarrassment, during my last two years, of the Friday night dances. There were no men to dance with and for a couple of hours, we females circled the great hall, clasped bosom to bosom, in couples. As one of the taller girls I was always expected to dance 'man'. This not only ruined my ball-room dancing for ever but, allied to being cast as juvenile male lead in the Dramatic Society's end-of-term production of "Berkeley Square", it aroused my mother's worst fears. In a desperate attempt to try and preserve my femininity she showered me with glamorous underwear and frilly blouses, which were the envy of all my room-mates.

She had no cause for alarm on this score: my overwhelming revulsion as my super-sized headmistress clasped me firmly to her ample flesh and propelled me, masterfully, around the dance floor, (she was somewhat taller than I and so automatically took the lead,) was a sensation that, even today, fills me with nausea. There was no escaping this experience, even 'though, in accordance with protocol, no girl was allowed spontaneously, to invite the headmistress to dance.

Her partners were all carefully selected beforehand, by the Head Prefect and their names inscribed in a neatly-written dance programme, presented to her at the start of the evening's revelry and worn, tucked into the V of her dress, with a clean handkerchief. When the band struck up, no girl could start dancing until the headmistress had ceremoniously, permitted herself to take the floor, with her appointed partner. Contrary to true Royal etiquette however, it was the girl's responsibility to initiate the conversation. Looking back on it all, the Headmistress must have had outsize tolerance to feign genuine interest when, as a stock opening gambit, she was asked to comment, a dozen or so times at every dance, on the hockey or lacrosse team's prospects in the match, the following day.

I became obsessed with the necessity of avoiding the agony of those Friday night dances. Eventually, tone-deaf as I was, I talked myself into an audition for one of the school's two dance bands, and was appointed drummer.

The Headmistress contrived other opportunities of rating her sixth-formers social graces, such as little intimate dinner parties, held in the exclusive atmosphere of her private apartment. Every week, three senior girls were summoned to dine, fortified with a glass of sherry and, after coffee, offered the choice of playing Bridge, listening to classical records or having their horoscopes told.

The choice was rarely in doubt: the opportunity of hearing the hostess relate to each guest in turn, details of her character and potentialities, worked out partly through her personal knowledge and partly from her large, expensive book on astrology, was too good to miss. Moreover, she could never resist spicing the information with some of her own opinions which introduced fine personal undertones to the operation.

As far as my zodiac signs went, as a Geminian, I had no complaints; the sign of the Heavenly Twins augured well enough for my chosen career, too well for my Headmistress who, from the beginning, had disapproved, most heartily, of my ideas:

"A journalist, my dear! Surely you mean a writer, like Mary?" had been her initial shocked reaction. I had no intention of trying to emulate Mary Hayley-Bell, the dramatist and our most famous old girl, nor the much-lauded Doreen Wallace, the novelist who had preceded her. I wanted nothing of their lonely pen-pushing. I aimed to work on a newspaper, reporting the day's news as it happened, a woman writing her way into a man's world.

Now, it seemed, even the stars were endorsing my choice by appointing Mercury, the Winged Messenger of the Gods, as my ruler.

"Change and variety are the spice of life, to June people," replayed my Headmistress, I suspected, rather reluctantly. "But beware!" and she scrutinised me over her spectacles. ("Here it comes," I thought). "Beware of being 'Jack of all trades and Master of none' or, of 'Falling between two stools'. Remember, you can't 'Have your cake and eat it'!"

At the last end-of-term ball, she proffered some even stronger advice. It came after, true to the School's tradition, she had opened the ball by abandoning protocol: instead of waiting for one of the girls to invite her to dance, as soon as the band struck up for the first dance, she had risen majestically from her seat and, the focus of every eye, had swept across the room, like a ship in full sail, her long, chiffon skirts, billowing behind her, to choose her partner. Down the hall she strode, while the girls watched, breathless with excitement, until she stopped before the one she had selected to be her next year's Head Prefect and, to near-hysterical applause swept her blushing, trembling choice into a Victory Waltz.

Afterwards, she danced with each of her old prefects in turn, a farewell dance, because we were leaving the following morning. My turn came early in the evening, before I retreated to play the drums. I gritted my teeth, preparing for the moment of physical contact with her for the very last time. But, for once, she danced well apart, staring me in the face.

"Good luck!" she said, "if you insist on pursuing your inappropriate career. But there's one piece of advice I would like to offer you: whatever you do, my dear, don't get married; you're just not the type."

Over the years, my husband, from time to time, has certainly been inclined to agree!

★ ★ ★

The first real encouragement to pursue my "inappropriate career" came from a most unexpected source; from a simple soul who my autocratic grandfather once described, affectionately as "the ugliest woman he had ever met." He said it to her face, but she only smiled, as if he were paying her a compliment. Indeed, to Jane Hill, to be noticed at all, was something of a compliment.

She was the old-fashioned family retainer who joined my grandparent's household after her unfortunate lapse from grace, when she was eighteen years old. This unmentionable episode resulted in a son she had never seen and was recalled mainly by a set of soldier's buttons, kept in an old tea-caddy, among her treasures in the glass-fronted corner cupboard in her kitchen.

For as long as I can remember, it was called "Jane's Kitchen", in recognition perhaps of all her years of faithful, selfless service, in atonement for her one mortal sin. As a token of her well-earned tenancy and, as a symbol of the family's appreciation, she had, very graciously, been allowed to choose the wallpaper.

It had been an inspired choice; a blaze of flamboyant cabbage roses, rioting over a garden trellis, perhaps a brave, if wistful reminder of her own brief summer. But it gave the room a warmth and intimacy, emphasised by the copper kettle, shining on the hearth in front of the little open fire. The kettle was always kept just off the simmer, ready to brew up a "nice cup of tea".

This was the only cooking permitted in "Jane's Kitchen". The rest, with the washing and other household chores, was done in the adjoining scullery. There, at the large, white kitchen sink, as a little girl, I had screamed in furious protest, as my grandfather held my head under the cold water tap to "wash away my willfullness".

Afterwards, I sobbed it out of me, on Jane's ample lap, cradled against her starched apron, soothed by the aroma of the strong linament she rubbed into her rheumaticky joints. Later on, she made both of us "a nice cup of tea", her unfailing remedy for everything.

Over the years, whenever I was troubled, I would make an excuse to escape from my grandparents' gentle sitting-room conversation and slip into "Jane's Kitchen" and her greeting, "Kettle's just boiling. Tea won't be a minute!"

"They tell me you want to be a journalist," she said, as I sat sipping a mouthful of the strong, sweet stuff, when I was about sixteen. "Can't say I know exactly what that means, but if you're sure you know what you're about, I'll look into it if you like."

I gulped the tea, so quickly it burnt my throat. This was quite something: the first time Jane had offered this important service to me, and with it came a sudden feeling of inevitability.

"That's right," I said, as casually as I could. "Please do. Please do look into it."

To "Look Into It", as far as Jane Hill was concerned, meant a journey, on two buses, to visit her friend, Mrs Morley. It was a half-day's outing. As soon as the lunch things had been cleared away, Jane would appear at the sitting-room door, looking strangely unfamiliar in her best black coat and skirt, instead of frock and apron, and her black felt boater, firmly secured with innumerable hat-pins onto her artificially padded-out roll of hair.

"Just off to see Mrs Morley, Ma'am. Shan't be long:" she would announce, portentiously, and my grandmother would nod her approval. Some four hours later, Jane would be back, heavy with the responsibility of bearing Mrs Morley's pronouncement on whatever had been the subject of the consultation.

On arriving at Mrs Morley's, there would have been a cup of tea and a chat, during which Jane would have explained the purpose of her visit. Then, the tea-things cleared away, it would be time for business: with due ceremony,

Jane would have been invited to "Cut the Cards" to reveal the inevitable outcome of the matter under consideration.

It was an infallible method of fortune-telling, one that long before I was born, had been proved conclusively, as I was never tired of hearing. My mother's wedding was the cause at stake. It was to be a big wedding; three hundred invitations had been sent out and the final preparations were well under way when the bride, it seemed, began to have serious misgivings about her 'intended'. However, eve-of-wedding nerves were common enough in those days and no-one paid very much attention: except Jane. It was the first real wedding she had been involved in and she could not believe this beloved bride should be entering matrimony any less radiantly or less confidently than all the story-book brides in the two-penny magazines, stuffed under the cushion of her old armchair. Perplexed and concerned, she consulted Mrs Morley.

On her return, she reported straight to my grandfather.

"She'll never marry the man she's

engaged to," she said, and I could picture her round, earnest face, gleaming with concern. "Mrs Morley's quite certain. She cut the cards twice, to make sure. She says, even if she walks down the aisle, she'll never marry him."

My grandfather must have been furious. Until then, he had tolerated Mrs Morley's prognoses, with amused good-humour. But this was the end. He warned her messenger, in no uncertain terms, to keep such rubbish to herself and, on pain of death, never to mention Mrs Morley's name again.

I can imagine how Jane received my grandfather's threats. Staring up at him, disdainfully, from her height of just over five feet, hearing him out and then marching from the room. They confirmed the healthy disrespect she had for all men, since her own unfortunate experience. Whether or not she obeyed my grandfather, was her secret, but one week later, the bride, despite her parent's respective tears and fury, wrote to her bridegroom calling the whole thing off. By the same post, she wrote a secret note to a gay bachelor, nearly twenty years her senior. A year later they were married, she and the middle aged-man who was to be my father.

Nearly twenty years later, Jane was at it again:

"Mrs Morley says you'll be a journalist," she declared, as she pulled out her hat-pins, removed her hat and carefully poked the pins through the headband, ready for the hat's next outing. She rubbed the mark the hat had left on her forehead, reflectively. There was more to come:

"Mrs Morley says, as it's the first time I've cut the cards for you, you just might not believe it really will come true. So she's sent you a proof she can see into the future." I waited, expecting at any moment, to see a mysterious genie or a white rabbit, emerge from Jane's black, leather handbag.

But Mrs Morley didn't work that way.

"You'll have proof soon," Jane nodded, knowingly. "Mrs Morley sees you mixed up in some money matters. It'll be before the next new moon. You'll know she's right because of the man with a finger missing, on his right hand." I had a feeling of anti-climax: Mrs Morley probably imbibed the same staple diet of two-penny magazines as Jane did!

Two weeks later, in the Post Office, there was a new cashier behind the counter where I went to withdraw some money from my saving's account. He pushed the notes towards me, through the bars. The top portion of his first finger was missing. It was his right hand.

Over the years there were other instances of Mrs Morley's powers, but never more propitious than when she intervened for the last time, from beyond the grave. This was ten years after my grandfather's death when Jane had assumed responsibility for the well-being of my dear, beautiful little grandmother, whom she adored. For the first few years, she coped with running the big house on her own, but gradually her health deteriorated and, despite all her protestations, it was necessary to engage a series of younger, so-called assistant-housekeepers, to help her.

They came and went, in rapid succession, largely because Jane deeply resented sharing her kitchen with any of them. Suddenly, it was obvious it was no longer a question of sharing, she would have to hand over entirely. From her hospital bed, she summoned the sparse, elderly spinster, who had inherited it and was already wondering if she had taken on rather too big a responsibility. Jane left her in no doubt:

"I have a message to give you," she announced, fixing her visitor with a baleful eye. "It's from a friend of mine who's gone ahead and who I'll be seeing shortly," she went on, with a reverent glance towards the ceiling.

"My friend, Mrs Morley, says I'm to tell you that, whatever happens, you're to look after the Missus for the rest of her life. It's your solemn duty. If you fail, Mrs Morley says it'll be the worse for you."

Mrs Morley or Divine Inspiration? It came to the same thing: my dependent little grandmother acquired another loyal retainer, for the rest of her long life.

★ ★ ★

24

"Getting your first job as a journalist is the most difficult job you'll ever have to do," said Tom Clarke, one of the toughest men in the newspaper business and my Tutor in Practical Journalism at King's College, London University and it was a warning he repeated at regular intervals during the two years' Diploma Course.

"For you," he said, eyeing me pityingly at the end of my last term, "it will be virtually an impossibility."

I stood, suitably humbled, before the wisdom and experience of this famous editor of the old *News Chronicle* who had been trained in Manchester, won his newspaper spurs in China and Australia and made his name in Fleet Street and who now scrutinised me, over the top of his glasses with the rather dubious look of a journalist about to abandon a rather seedy news story.

"It beats me," he went on, "why, just twelve months ago you were rated the most promising girl student in the year — and now, this."

"THIS" was total failure in the final examinations in economics, history, literature and current affairs: in fact in every subject of the Diploma Course except Tom Clarke's own subject, practical journalism, which I had passed with flying colours. That, it seemed, did little to mitigate the sorry state of affairs:

"Tragic," he murmured, "just goes to show you can never trust a filly . . . "

I responded with a rather horsey snort and then, fearing I had gone too far, blew my nose vigorously. Suddenly he was embarrassingly paternal, his face softening with genuine concern, "Well," he said, "what went wrong?"

"Oh, this and that," I countered and gulped back the urge to explain about an ill-fated time-consuming spring-time romance with a gay medical student.

"Well, you realise that we can't, in all honesty, do anything to help you to get a job," he announced, almost apologetically, "though I must admit," he added, "you'd have made a first-rate journalist; you still can if you've got enough in you to go out and talk yourself into a good job, which isn't easy without a reference."

The word "reference" rang a bell;

somewhere, in the dim and distant past I remembered hearing our old family doctor, encouraging me to be a writer and telling me of another patient of his, a very famous lady novelist who offered to help me find a job when the time came.

"I'll get a job," I told my tutor, with sudden and unreasonable conviction. That very night I wrote off to my dearly beloved Dr Friend.

His reply came within a week; a brief acknowledgement of my letter enclosing with it an envelope, addressed in unfamiliar large, flowing handwriting, to the editor of the top woman's fashion magazine. It was unsealed. It contained a friendly, informal note from the famous novelist asking the editor if she could manage to find a place for an "ambitious, capable and highly imaginative" young journalist friend. I crossed my fingers, sealed the letter and decided to deliver it in person.

The magazine was situated on the top two floors of a smart office block just off Bond Street. I stepped out of the smoothly-running lift into a world of pale blue carpets, exquisite flower arrangements, subdued lighting and discreet quietness. Nothing could have been further removed, in the world of journalism, from the noise and bustle of a newspaper office. A softly-spoken receptionist enquired my business:

"I should like to see the Editor, please."

"Have you an appointment?"

"I'm afraid not."

"What is it about?"

"It's a sort of personal matter . . . "

As if on cue, a door opened and a rather plain, perfectly-groomed, middle-aged woman emerged and swept up to the reception desk. She was a study in under-stated elegance and looked as if she had come straight from the hairdressers, the beauticians and the dieticians, before slipping into a simple little expensive suit, designed for the successful career woman. I suddenly remember I was overdue for a hair-do.

"I'm out for the rest of the morning, dear. If anyone calls put them through to Leslie," the elegant creature told the receptionist.

"Yes, of course. Actually, this young lady was just asking if she could see you."

I stepped forward and intercepted my future editor, before she could forestall me.

"I brought you this letter," I said.

The perfectly-arched eyebrows lifted, in sudden surprise, as their owner scrutinised me, momentarily startled at the unheralded intrusion. Then, recovering her poise she bestowed a toothy smile, accepted the blue envelope and tore it open.

"Well I never," she said, in genuine delight, "it's from Vicky. Dear Vicky! How is she?"

"She's fine," I said and fervently hoped it was true.

"It's simply ages since I saw her," she confided, as she perused the note.

"Not nearly as long ago as I did," I thought to myself, conjuring up a mental picture of the eton-cropped, trousered celebrity I knew only from newspaper photographs. How came she to be accepted in this place of femininity?

She was more than accepted; she was all powerful:

"If Vicky says you should have a job here, then I'm sure you should," said the Editor. "We can talk about it on the way down in the lift."

She rang the bell; the lift doors opened silently, we stepped inside; she touched the button with an elegantly-manicured finger and by the time the doors opened again at the ground floor it had been arranged that I should collect a set of fashion photos later in the day and try my hand as a caption writer. It was the smoothest ride I had ever had!

"Do remember me to Vicky," she cooed, as she disappeared up Bond Street.

That was on Friday. On Sunday afternoon I lay back on the cushions of a rowing boat, moored on the Thames and thumbed through the set of fashion stills for the hundredth time, waiting for inspiration, my head on the shoulder of my current boyfriend. He tried his best to be helpful:

"Tonight she'll tip-toe in a cloud of

chiffon . . . " he murmured, studying a photo of a model in a flowing ball-gown.

I stared at him: I'd never realised he was the romantic type.

"Great!" I encouraged, scribbling down the words, "Just carry on."

"Tomorrow, in spots before his eyes, she'll dazzle him to distraction . . . " he proferred, for the caption to a girl in an outfit of black and white polka dots.

"Gosh!" I said, "you're really marvellous."

"Then marry me?" he said.

"No, thanks," I said, "journalism doesn't go with marriage."

"Don't worry," he said. "You'll grow out of it."

"Never," I said, with burning indignation. "I promise you, here and now, I never will."

"We'll see," he said, with infuriating certainty. "I'll give you a year."

"A year for what?"

"To get it out of your system."

"You're wasting your time. I'll never change." And I never did. But eventually we were married just the same.

Meanwhile, the woman Editor was

delighted with the captions although they were the first and last I was ever asked to write. But, no matter, they justified me being given a job as an assistant editorial assistant at a modest salary of £3 a week. My chief responsibility was to translate copy from the American edition of the magazine into more acceptable English so that "clothes for the Fall" was changed to read "clothes for the Autumn" and phrases like "candy stripes" and "gasolene blue" were similarly Anglosised.

"It's just a beginning," they assured me, something to fill in time while "you get the feel of things". And while I was "imbibing the atmosphere" they suggested I might also like to take down and type a few letters for the editorial assistant. I was willing to do this until I discovered that most of her letters were destined for the Paris office and were dictated in French. As a translator I felt I had better stick to American.

"Getting the feel of things" also included going to fashion shows to swell the ranks of the magazine's contingent so that we occupied a prestigious share of the little gold chairs in the crowded salons. There, equipped with a new note-book I eventually recorded my first impressions:

"OH YOU FAT, UGLY WOMEN WHO SIT AT DRESS SHOWS, PERSPIRING PROFUSELY, WITH YOUR LEGS WIDE APART! WHAT BUSINESS HAVE YOU TO COMMENT ON FASHION?" I scribbled idly during the third show of a hot July day. I was sitting in the second row, between the Editorial Assistant and the Merchandising Assistant, squashed, according to protocol, behind the Fashion Editor and the Beauty Editor who occupied the best seats in the room, right in the centre of the front row.

"My dear," hissed the Editorial Assistant, her eye rivetted on my initial inspiration, "that's not at all the way we write things."

"No," I said, "I'm sure not." I closed my note-book, but the boredom was already setting in: boredom at talking, thinking, writing about clothes, every single moment of the day and, because of the time-lag in producing the magazine, always at least three months in advance of when any of them were likely to be worn. I seemed to be caught up in a gigantic machine whose job was to create, foster and then satisfy an interest in fashion, over and over again.

Moreover I felt curiously lonely, as the odd one out among the carefully groomed women and the even more beautifully coiffeured men with the inevitable red carnation in the buttonhole of their extravagantly-waisted pin-stripes, their high, drawling voices and their sickening perfume.

It was not 'till years later that I learned they were some of the most rewarding men to work with; sensitive and sympathetic and artistic and who, unlike more masculine male colleagues, did not spend the journeys to and from our assignments indulging in interminable accounts of their unsatisfactory marriages or subjecting me to soul-searching confessions about their sexual frustrations. Only with maturity, did I learn that there could be no better companions than these ageless "boys": they could chatter on about the theatre or antiques or paintings; knew just where to buy the very type of curtain materials I wanted; noticed if I had happened to change my perfume and could always be relied on to produce a new recipe for me to try out at my next dinner party. More important, I could relax in their company knowing that, after a day's working camaraderie, there would be no danger of having to fend off the inevitable pass, somewhere on the way home.

But at that stage I was as intolerant of them as I soon was of the whole world of the fashion magazine: I was only in my working element once or twice a week, after office hours when, to eke out my earnings, I covered London assignments for the *Yorkshire Evening News*, sending them reports of any events that concerned my fellow Yorkshiremen.

I had a "roving commission". I combed the advertisements and social diaries for any business, professional or social functions of Yorkshire interest, kept an eye open for Yorkshire after-dinner speakers and followed the movements of the local M.P.s like a ferret. The London branch of the Society of Yorkshiremen had never known such publicity as they suddenly received. But I was hungry in more ways than one and a good dinner, followed immediately by a dash to King's Cross station to post my report of the speech in the late-night mail box to be delivered in the Leed's office of the newspaper first thing in the morning and appear, impressively by-lined "By our London Correspondent", in the lunch-time edition of the paper, offered a reward in excess of payment at the rate of 3½d. a line.

It was my responsibility to decide which events to cover and organise the invitations; but sometimes I slipped up. Like the time I saw a crowd collected on the pavement outside a building in Lower Regent Street and, on enquiring, learned they were waiting to see the arrival of a fashionable young author who was lecturing there that afternoon. Suddenly, I remembered hearing that he was a Yorkshireman. I checked with one of his waiting fans. He was, but, she assured me, there was not the slightest hope of getting in, without a ticket. The burly commissionaire endorsed this.

In those days, when authors could be

almost as big a draw as pop groups and film stars, it seemed that my hopes of getting into the lecture and writing a report were in jeopardy, particularly as at that stage in my career I could not even produce a Press card. From the back of the crowd I glimpsed the idol's arrival; he acknowledged his fans, disappeared into the hall and the crowds dispersed. The commissionaire shrugged his shoulders and went off. I remembered the advice of my Tutor in Practical Journalism and slipped round to the back of the building and found the fire-escape.

Two floors up and the fire-escape passed conveniently alongside a large, frosted sash window which was open a few inches at the top and bottom: it moved quietly and easily. But as it slid open there was an outbreak of tumultuous applause. I ducked hastily but, as I did, I glimpsed row upon row of the backs of people's heads and realised with relief the applause was not for me but for the famous author, away in the distance on the platform, beyond the heads, who was just rising to his feet to begin his address. No-one even noticed me as I hoisted myself onto the sill and dropped quietly over into the audience. Like most good stories, it was just a matter of timing.

Many years later we met again, the author and I, in a regional television studio where he had come to be interviewed about his latest book and where it was apparent that he had not managed to withstand the passage of time quite as well as his writings. In such a small studio, a trained make-up girl was not on hand, so that when the balding author produced a blonde toupée and asked if there was someone who could fix it on for him? I had to send for one of the secretaries who invariably coped with such emergencies.

Unfortunately, the author had forgotten to bring the fixative for his toupée, but the resourceful secretary was unperturbed; she disappeared and returned with a white, sticky-looking substance in a little bowl, dabbed it along his hair-line and on the edge of his toupée and it did the job nicely — so nicely, in fact, that he never even bothered to remove the toupée after the show, just thanked us, put on his hat and went off. The secretary sighed deeply as he disappeared through the door.

"Tired?" I said.

"No, relieved," she giggled. "That's the first toupée I've ever had to put on."

"Lucky we had the stuff for sticking on."

"We hadn't," she said. "That's why I'm so relieved he didn't want me to take it off. It's fixed on with some of that everlasting adhesive, guaranteed to last a life-time."

I felt suddenly guilty, as if I should have taken more care of the old author who, twenty years before, albeit unknowingly, had, quite literally tempted me to climb out of the fashion world to become involved in the sort of journalism I really loved.

★ ★ ★

A provincial evening newspaper, such as the old *Yorkshire Evening News*, publishing five different editions between noon and seven-thirty in the evening, is the best possible training ground for any aspiring journalist. An imaginative editor, all for trying out something new and with quite a reputation as a "lady's man" agreed to give his "Special London Correspondent" a month's trial as a staff reporter.

One of my earliest responsibilities meant arriving at the office at seven o'clock in the morning, with the office cleaners and reading through the national morning papers, marking as I did so, in red pencil, all the stories with any Yorkshire significance.

At eight-thirty, the burly Scottish News Editor, would arrive, light up his pipe and go through all my stories. He would decide at a glance, which to discard and which justified further investigation, with a view to doing follow-up stories on them, in the evening paper.

In due course, two or three of the least promising ones were passed back to me to "look into"; others were allocated, according to their merits, to my male colleagues, as they arrived, from nine o'clock onwards, in reverse order of precedence: thus, the deputy News Editor, who usually strolled in last of all, would find all the cuttings pertaining to the big "lead story" of the day, neatly arranged on his desk, waiting for his attention.

My arrival, in the Reporters' Room represented a shocking start to the week, in every sense: at first, I was treated with a mixture of mock courtesy and tolerant amusement, by the eight or so men in the office; but amusement spiced with suspicion at a female's intrusion into their rough man's world.

"You won't stick it, kid!" they confided to me, in turn, each in a different way.

Not that I was the first female journalist in the paper; primly ensconsed, behind a little glass partition, in the farthest corner, was a spinsterish Scottish lady with a black fringe. It was her job to write up the wedding reports and an occasional fashion show. Very jealous she was, of her responsibility. But as far as I was concerned, she had no cause for alarm; her well-insulated preserve was the last place I coveted.

Neither had I any qualms about being able to stick the life as a "straight reporter": every time I pushed open the swing door from the street and climbed the first few stone steps up to the office, I inhaled, deeply and satisfyingly, the strange, unmistakable, pungent smell of news-type and paper and printer's ink, the intoxicating flavour of every newspaper office I would ever know. I sensed that this was the one elixir I would never tire of; it greeted me, almost comfortingly, when I returned, down-cast, after failing to get my story and mindful of my News Editor's warning;

"Come back with the story, or don't come back at all."

I would gulp huge, heady lung-fulls of it as I chased triumphantly up the stairs, two at a time, having beaten an opponent on the rival newspaper, to the earlier edition. Eventually, whenever I started a new job on another newspaper, the same spicey, familiar smell would be there, on the strange stairway leading to an unknown Reporters' Room, waiting to reassure me that these steps were just a logical progression.

But it was on this first, Yorkshire, newspaper, that I learnt a discipline that was to stand me in good stead for life.

It entailed remembering, when out on a story, to make a mental note of the position of the nearest telephone, before starting work, to be sure of being able to beat the other reporters to it, when the time came to 'phone the story back to the paper. I learnt too, to compose a story over the telephone, straight from the shorthand notes, dictating it, down to the last comma and capital letter, to a speed typist who could type faster than I could talk. Afterwards I never tired of the thrill of buying a paper on the street corner and standing in a doorway to read my story, set out in the cold authority of newsprint, before I had a chance to get back to the office.

To miss the first possible edition or to return unduly late from a job was cause for an inquest the next day. As for serious mistakes: it was an unwritten law that every reporter was permitted to make only one.

One day, after telephoning a report from a neighbouring town, I stopped, on the way back, at a famous inn to have a drink with some of the other reporters and cameramen. As always with newspapermen, the talk flowed, even more freely than the beer. After about an hour, the inn-keeper came over.

"The young lady's wanted on the telephone," he announced. As far as I knew, no-one in the world knew of my whereabouts. But I had underestimated my News Editor:

"How did you know I was here?" I asked.

"Every reporter I've ever known, who's travelled that road has stopped at that pub on the way home," he grumbled. "But you've wasted enough time for one day. Just leave those idle fellows and come straight back. There's another job waiting."

For months, my main job was reporting funerals and inquests. There was an endless, depressing stream of them and as my current boy-friend was a coffin manufacturer, with a weather-eye open for an influenza epidemic, I acquired a somewhat fatalistic view of life. In the case of funerals, I would stand at the cemetery gates so the mourners, as they passed, could mutter their names to me in suitably hushed tones or hand me their visiting cards. Some gave me their own cards and announced they were really there to represent someone completely different which, back in the office, took a bit of sorting out.

The inquests, once I'd schooled myself to approach them impersonally, were pleasant enough, chiefly because of the understanding that was soon established with the Coroner, a tall, gaunt gentleman, completely bald, who was known, affectionately, by the Press as "Old Death's Head". He could invariably be relied upon for a few pithy comments, good enough to ensure the report of the proceedings made the final editions. Before uttering these immortal pronouncements he would usually pause a moment and glare at me to make sure I was giving him my full attention and then, slowly, as if he were afraid of over-taxing my limited shorthand, would address his remarks to me, deliberately and meaningfully.

Our nice understanding was furthered when he insisted on escorting me back to the office, regaling me, on the short walk, with tales about bigger and better inquests than any I had yet seen, like the one about the poor chap who put his head on the railway line.

"When I saw his body at the inquest," the Coroner said, "my police sergeant had laid him out all nice and tidy. I just couldn't see a thing wrong with him.

"I said to the sergeant 'Funny way for a chap to smarten himself up, before deciding to do himself in,' and made my point my giving a little tug at the elegantly-tied muffler, round his neck.

"Would you believe it, his head just topped over. The muffler had been the sergeant's inspiration, to tidy things up a bit. But, for a moment, he gave me quite a shock, I can tell you."

I laughed, loud and appreciatively, 'though inwardly I felt slightly sick; perhaps I was not yet quite as tough as I ought to be!

Finally, the inquests ceased and I made it, at last, onto the Press bench in the Police Courts. If I had been considered a novelty in the Reporters' Room, it was nothing compared to the surprise the arrival of a woman reporter created in the musty court-room of the centuries-old

Leeds Town Hall. Policemen grinned; solicitors nudged each other and winked and there came a day when the crusty old Stipendiary Magistrate refused to allow the solicitor in a particularly sordid case of sexual assault, to continue with his prosecution until "that young lady" had left the court-room.

As the young lady in question, I was the only reporter from my paper in court at the time, so I sat firm. There followed a whispered consultation between the Stipendiary and the Clerk to the Court and a more senior reporter, from another newspaper, was called up to join in. Eventually with much clearing of his throat, the Stipendiary announced that he had been advised that, to all intents and purposes, the Press was Sexless, and the young lady was at liberty to remain. My grinning companions on the Press bench, clapped their thumbnails together, in silent applause and recorded the story of the interruption as a humorous-relief paragraph, for their respective papers. For once I didn't try and compete.

By this time, back at the office, however, I at last seemed to have been accepted by my colleagues as one of them, a fully-fledged newspaper reporter, sharing the fun and the responsibilities. Or thought I was one of them, until the incident of the chair.

The office boasted an odd assortment of chairs, mostly wooden upright ones with leather seats, sometimes with cushions or a pile of newspapers on top, to raise them to a more comfortable height for the typewriter. I had never really thought about my chair until the day when someone remarked casually;

"Better get a cushion for that chair or it'll make your skirt as shiny as our trousers."

"That would never do! Whatever is the office coming to!" another exclaimed, with mock sarcasm.

"Give her your chair then, Jim." Suddenly, in the outbreak of banter, the young red-haired sports writer marched across to my desk with his chair, and changed it for mine.

"Leave it. I don't want it," I muttered, hanging onto my chair, fiercely determined to stamp on the slightest sign of sexual discrimination. But he insisted. The next morning, arriving, as usual, first in the office, I swopped the chairs back again.

But that was not the end of the story: about a week later, the matter was re-opened by none less than the Senior Reporter:

"About your chair . . . " he began, rather formally.

"What about it?"

"We really feel that it's not right you should have one of the worst chairs in the office. So, we've done a bit of negotiating and have arranged a little surprise for you. It should be here later today."

It was: a tall semi-occasional armchair with walnut arms and legs, the stiff back and seat padded in a rather sickly shade of apple-green brocade.

"The darlings!" I thought, tenderly, looking at it with well-concealed horror. They'd gone to these ridiculous lengths, I suppose, just to show that at least they'd decided to accept a woman reporter into their office. It was a great moment!

"Try it. See how it feels," they urged, crowding round, delighted with themselves.

Like a queen, ascending her throne,

I graciously obliged. They fell about, laughing.

"It suits her, it really does," they congratulated each other.

"Do you like it?"

"Is it comfortable?"

"Have another look."

I stood up again and prodded the upholstery. I much preferred the inconspicuous old one, but if this was what they wanted . . .

"Look closer," they said, and with the air of producing a white rabbit out of a hat, one of them, with a flourish, lifted up the seat. It was a commode.

There was a sudden silence, while I felt my face slowly turning a deep red. So they had not accepted me, after all; this was their way of saying a newspaper office had no place for a woman reporter.

"Thank you all very much," I said, closing the lid. "It was a nice thought." I sat down and busied myself, sorting through some papers.

"It's just a joke," they said, "You don't mind? You're not annoyed?"

"Of course not," I lied. "It's just the

job. Might even come in handy one of these days."

One by one, they drifted away. I waited until they had all gone, tidied up my desk and left the office. So perhaps the older generation had been right, after all, and journalism was not a suitable job for a woman.

But the next morning, the strange, newspapery smell on the stairs seemed sweeter than ever. Whatever they said or did, I intended to stay, even if I had to sit it out on a hideous green commode. I steeled myself and pushed open the door of the office. And then I saw it: at my desk, in place of the offensive piece of furniture, stood a neat little wooden arm-chair, upholstered in flowered green rep. Pinned to the back was a note:

"We like a bit of skirt — but not a shiny one!"

"I love it," I yelled, as they came in, one by one, and added, with bravado, "shame the seat doesn't lift!"

By that time, as far as stories went, I was taking my chance with the rest. One evening, when I was just about to leave the office, the News Editor called me over to his desk:

"This is on your way home," he said, handing me a slip of paper with a name and address.

"This chap's been 'phoning up all day. Says he's a doctor and has a very important story to tell us, which is too hot to talk about over the telephone. Would you call in and see if there's anything in it? He'll be expecting you."

It was the doctor's wife who opened the door to me. She looked somewhat distraught and showed me into the waiting-room, explaining her husband was just finishing his surgery. There was one patient, sitting in the waiting-room. He looked up expectantly, when the doctor appeared at the door to beckon me into the surgery. There, in urgent whispers, he confided that his story was so secret that he dare not mention it while even one single patient remained in the house. Would I please wait until he had dealt with the one remaining potential eavesdropper?

By this time, it had dawned on me that the worried doctor was something of a 'nut case'. I tried to placate him;

"Don't worry." I assured him. "There's no hurry. I'll take a short walk and come back a little later, when you've finished." It seemed the best way of making a quick get-away.

"You're like all the rest of them. You don't believe me," he flared up. "But, now you're here, I'm going to prove it to you, so just come in here."

There was no escape. He piloted me back to the waiting and the ever-hopeful patient. Apparently, whatever may have been the patient's trouble, he didn't suffer from nerves: he remained quite unperturbed and looked as if nothing unusual were happening, even when the doctor turned the key in the door and we were locked in.

"I'll teach you to doubt me," he shouted. "You'll be sorry you ever saw me, when I've finished with you."

He could say that again!

I heard his wife, trying to reason with him; there was a short argument; then silence.

There's an immediate feeling of intimacy about being locked up with another person, even a complete stranger.

53

"What's your particular trouble?" I enquired, solicitously, hoping to break the ice and find an ally.

"Ulcers," he replied, still staring, gloomily, at the carpet. "Do you think the doctor will be much longer?" There seemed no point in offering him false encouragement.

"If I were you, I'd forget all about seeing the doctor, and get out while the going's good," I advised, pushing open the window and estimating the possibility of a hasty, if unorthodox exit. The house was built on a slight hill and, although the waiting room was on the ground floor, the garden sloped away, so that the windows were about twelve feet above the ground. But there was plenty of creeper and a convenient drain-pipe. No sound could be heard, from outside the door.

"I'm afraid I'll have to go without seeing the doctor," I said.

My companion didn't look at all well, and I hesitated to try and persuade him to join me. On the other hand, it seemed wrong just to abandon him to a maniac. He made the decision himself.

"I'll have to wait," he said. "I need

some more pills from the doctor."

"Well, cheerio, then!" I said, one foot over the window-sill.

"Good-bye," he called, still quite unperturbed, as I lowered myself and, jumping clear, made my escape. He certainly didn't seem the type to have ulcers!

Later that evening, I telephoned the doctor's house: his wife answered the 'phone. No, she was sorry, her husband couldn't speak to me; he couldn't speak to me later; he had had a breakdown and been taken off to hospital.

Rather him than me, I thought, thankfully, as by that time, after a few months of married life, I was beginning to suspect I was slightly pregnant.

2

Domestic Digressions

"A woman who wants to write shouldn't marry, shouldn't have children: she should be a nun or a tramp!"

THESE sentiments, expressed by a fellow Yorkshirewoman, Storm Jameson, with the experience of a wife and mother, forty novels and nearly eighty years of living, was a rather more authoritative version of the sentiments voiced many years previously, by my buxom headmistress. But I was a Geminian; it was my birth-right to "have my cake and eat it", even if, in terms of producing a family and, at the same time, remaining a working journalist, it required, not only a sympathetic husband, but the professional help of no less than five gynaecologists. In their field, from a consumer point of view, I became

56

something of an expert.

The first one in my life was a cheery, no-nonsense type of fellow who looked like a retired rugby forward. Immediately he and my husband met, it turned out that that was exactly what he was and, for the remainder of their association, my interesting condition was relegated to one of quite secondary importance. Perhaps this was just as well; women journalists tend to have over-vivid imaginations and this treatment helped to restore the, to me, unbelievably, terrifying process of reproduction, to quite normal proportions. So did this consultant's ritual reassuring slap on my posterior, at the end of each pre-natal examination: a gentle gesture which, subconsciously, I suppose, might have been intended to indicate a rather fatherly relationship. In fact it had the very opposite effect and although, by no stretch of imagination, could he have been described as a "romantic figure", with the optimistic outlook of my profession somewhat exaggerated by my condition, I looked forward to our monthly assignations, with a delicious sense of expectancy, as if I were going on a sort of extra-marital blind date. As the months went by a "blind date" in the most literal sense, was certainly the only one I could have hoped for, unless of course, gynaecologists had different priorities from lesser men: which, in many ways, I rather suspect they have!

Anyway, the day after my eight-pound son was born, my cheery deliverer sat on the side of my bed and contemplated me with flattering intensity:

"This," he grinned appreciatively, "is one of the most rewarding moments of my work; seeing a new mother look ten years younger, overnight."

I smiled demurely. We clinked sherry glasses and, for one dreamy, disloyal moment, I contemplated calling our first-born "David" after him — except, the sudden change of plan would have required a bit of justifying, as far as my husband was concerned.

Nevertheless, disloyalty to the burly, sympathetic Leeds gynaecologist who had introduced me to the mysteries of motherhood, seemed absolutely out of the question the second time I was pregnant, even though by then we were living more than two hundred miles away. In any case, if the baby turned out to be another boy, it seemed hardly fair to deprive him of his elder brother's birthright — of being eligible to play cricket for Yorkshire. Surprisingly, my husband saw the logic of this argument and, just before his second son was due to make his appearance, we squashed ourselves and our two-year-old and all the paraphernalia, into a small car and returned to the country of women who had given birth to heroes like Sutcliffe and Hutton, Yardley and Truman.

I sensed however, that this sort of pilgrimage would soon have to stop: with two sons eligible to carry his name into the Yorkshire XI, my husband, quite understandably, felt he had made a sufficient token contribution to the sporting potential of his wife's native county and that, although in cricketing terms, we had been forced to make our home in a minor county, it was just possible that, even in that second-class environment, there was a first-class gynaecologist within striking distance!

There was: he was an elderly, professorial

type; quite brilliant, they said. As I outlined my long list of troubles, he rubbed his domed, bald head reflectively and peered at me through his spectacles, listening a little too earnestly and attentively for my own peace of mind, as if I were a most unusual specimen, causing him a good deal of perplexity.

All I wanted was to be reassured that I was the most normal of normal, but he pandered to my sense of the dramatic. Eyes closed, in rapt concentration, his long, thin fingers barely fluttered over my stomach, gleaning, with scarcely a touch, all the information he needed. Illogically, I felt uncomfortably sanctified, a lonely being apart and, quite irrationally, I longed for a friendly, reassuring flip on my behind, or an earthy joke or two, to keep things on a more basic level, as his rugger-playing predecessor would certainly have provided. At the miscarriage, he was solemn and quietly efficient and made me feel slightly guilty as if I had somehow let him down.

He retired soon afterwards, which was rather convenient and my next professional encounter was with an older edition of my first loved gynaecologist but, this time, he was a real father-figure; a gentle giant of a man, with an impish sense of humour. He knew, I felt, about all my maternal inadequacies and accepted them as just part of his responsibility. He steered me, wisely and comfortingly, through the internal effects of having two such loyalties as motherhood and a career, until the day he died.

My fourth gynaecologist was back in my own generation again. There was quite a smug satisfaction, after my third visit, in seeing him listed in a glossy magazine, as one of the ten obstetricians in the country with the best bedside manner. Having put my money on him, so to speak, he made me feel as if I had, most unexpectedly, drawn a horse in a sweep-stake and it had, quite wonderfully, turned out to be a winner. But when I ventured to congratulate him, at the next consultation, he almost choked with fury and murmured something about sueing the magazine in question, for a breach of professional etiquette. He never did however and he continued to sport a deep, red carnation in the lapel of his elegant pin-striped suit, a buttonhole which may well have been the start of his notoriety troubles.

I never remember seeing him without a red carnation in his buttonhole, except on the one occasion when he was scrubbed up for the operating theatre and was clad in green cap and overalls. The flowers were so uniform in shape that I began to suspect that they were artificial. But when I challenged him on this, he removed the one he was wearing and presented it to me, with a flourish. He was that sort of man, with a bedside manner to match: there were no rugger jokes nor bottom-slapping; he was far too sophisticated for such indulgences. Yet, for all his worldliness and gallantry he managed to make me feel, neither romantic, nor sanctified, nor young; but just a not-very-out-of-the-ordinary person; a mother with a career, an image which I very much appreciated.

Unfortunately, for geographical reasons again, we had to part and by this time, feeling a very old hand at the game, I met my fifth. For the first time, in such a relationship, he was younger than I, or I assumed he was, but in compensation for this, he seemed to be a combination of my first two well-beloved gynaecologists, in one. By that time, of course, my early pre-disposition towards medical men had been firmly channelled into a predilection towards gynaecologists, even though I strongly suspected, that, like psychiatrists, their rather special type of consultant-patient relationship was little more than a deliberately-acquired professional stock-in-trade.

But, what matter? Eventually, it is only the end product that counts and, as a career-mother, in the days of short-lived marriages, there was nothing amiss in being able to think back affectionately of five gynaecologists to one husband rather than, as was more often the case, of the other way round.

★ ★ ★

Soon after Number One Son was born, we left Yorkshire for Norfolk and a rather small, unprepossessing, little house which I never suspected would winter and summer us, year after year and, all the time we were growing older, would also be growing — into quite a large, very sprawling and rather ungracious family home.

The house kept pace with us, I suppose, because, with so many pre-occupations, neither of us ever found enough time to look for a better one and because, whenever it became over-crowded or too cramped for our growing interests, it seemed easier just to add another piece onto it.

It was fortunate, or perhaps the verdict of future students of architecture will be to the contrary, that when we originally acquired the modest little three-and-a-half bedroomed "desirable residence", it adjoined a large L-shaped paddock which we bought, reasonably enough, to protect our view. We never intended to allow the house to encroach on it — fourteen times, at the last count!

From the convenience point of view, the house works well, but from the aesthetic aspect, it must be puzzling for passers-by to see a large, ungainly place, incorporating at least half-a-dozen different architectural styles squashed into just one corner of a four-acre garden.

We never, for the first half-dozen or so extensions, visualised it as our permanent home: we had dreams of some-day, somewhere, finding a long, low, red-brick, picture-book house, set in the heart of the country, overlooking a trout stream or a quiet Broad or private lake . . . someday, when we had time to enjoy it and I could afford to be more than ten minutes away from the office and need not worry about taking the boys to school; or whether there was a reasonable bus service for the "au pair" and a fertile catchment area for a constant supply of daily helps. Meanwhile, convenience was everything.

The house was just a youngster when we bought it. As well as its three-and-a-half bedrooms it had a large living room, small dining room, a tiny kitchen and a built-in garage. It seemed an easy operation to turn this garage into a nursery by knocking a door through from the kitchen and re-placing the double garage doors with a bay window. Meanwhile a pre-fabricated double garage was installed at the far end of the paddock.

As it turned out, this first simple alteration to the house took far longer than any of the far more complicated subsequent additions. But, for the first and last time, when it was finished I was sorry to see the workmen go. They came from an easy-going firm of small builders which, in the days of post-war building restrictions, were prepared to do more than anyone else for the one hundred pounds permitted by the government, for this sort of operation.

The firm's system of supervision was delightfully lax: regularly as clockwork, between nine and nine-thirty every morning, the foreman paid a daily visit to the two workmen permanently employed on the job. Only on Fridays did he come back again; that was in the afternoon, when he brought their weekly pay packets, otherwise, there was no danger of his re-appearing to find his men gone from the site for an hour or two, on their own affairs — or on mine!

They were willing chaps; they did my

shopping, as well as their own and, if I found myself in a muddle, would always lend a hand and peel the potatoes, clean the shoes and of course, mind the baby, whenever I had to go out. I would just push the pram into the most sheltered corner of his slowly-emerging nursery and leave him to them.

"Good idea to get him used to the place from the beginning," they'd both agreed and for three carefree months solved all my baby-sitting problems, during the day-time.

For my son's part, this introduction to what was to prove a long line of custodians, was a relaxed and cheery one, accompanied as it was by a non-stop background of dance music from their radio and with a fistful of putty his for the asking. Ever afterwards, he greeted any strange person who came to look after him in my absence, with cheerful expectancy.

Alas, in the fullness of time, this first building operation came to an end and, soon afterwards, the arrival of a new baby meant the beginning of an era of living-in helps, to leave me free to take up part-time newspaper work again. From all over Europe they came: a rosy-cheeked shy country girl from the Swiss mountains; a pair of over-confident German frauleins who could scarcely disguise their contempt that this particular housewife's place was not, primarily, in the house; a Finnish girl who smoked cigars in her bedroom before coming down to breakfast and a beautiful blue-eyed Austrian, with dark hair, who left rather suddenly because she discovered she was slightly pregnant. They had all come prepared to help to look after a baby and a toddler, mainly in return for learning to speak English.

The only snag was that, as far as I was concerned, the purpose of their presence in the household was to leave me free to go out. This meant that, for most of the day, there was no-one for them to talk English to except a baby and a toddler who spoke mainly unintelligible gibberish as a result, according to the latest psychological theory, of having a mother who had been too busy to spend much time indulging in baby talk, when changing his nappies. Ultimately, in his case the conglomeration of distorted European phraseology, superimposed on his pigeon English, took a good deal of sorting out.

We struggled on however, until the day when I came home from the office to find the current au pair locked up in her bedroom, having hysterics and my sons sitting outside the door, proudly clasping the key: they had apparently teased the poor girl, until she had threatened she would leave them and, to show she meant business, had gone up to her room to pack, whereupon they had decided they had better prevent such a disaster as this happening until I got home. That was the night we decided to muster our resources and acquire an English Nanny.

This great British institution certainly relieved me of maternal responsibilities — after I had done all the housework, most of the cooking and all the shopping. I was then free to go to the office with a clear conscience, confident that, with her little downy moustache and stiff white apron, any men, however young were absolutely safe with her.

Only once did I see her retreat: it

was on Sunday afternoon when we were having family tea round the nursery table. The fire crackled companionably and we ate hot, buttered toast and brown boiled eggs, laid by our own hens. We had collected the eggs that afternoon, as evidence of our attempt at pursuing a fundamental way of life in rural suburbia. The message, it seemed, had got home:

"Why don't our eggs have baby chicks in them?" enquired our elder son, getting nicely down to elementals.

Nanny seized the opportunity to take command:

"Because we haven't got a Daddy bird to give the Mummy bird the seed for a baby chick," she announced with text-book precision.

"How does the Daddy bird give the Mummy bird the seed?" he enquired logically.

Nanny sought valiantly to remember what the text-book had said, before passing the indescribeable over to my husband. He accepted the challenge nonchalantly:

"Oh, he just sits on her," he said airily and then, deciding to get the question over once and for all, added for good measure, "like a gentleman sits on a lady if they want to make a baby."

My son stopped eating his egg. This was quite something. He weighed the matter up.

"You mean as a Daddy sits on a Mummy?"

"Yes, exactly."

He stared his father straight in the eye, man to man stuff.

"What happens if a Daddy sits on another lady — like a Nanny?" I waited, eagerly. But my better-half had not commanded a platoon of Indian troops in Burma, without being able to cope with most contingencies. He did not flinch.

"Son," he said portentously, if a shade regretful, "Daddies just do not sit on other ladies, not ever." But his son had heard the lack of conviction.

"Why not?" he persisted, "A Nanny's a lady, isn't she?"

At that point the subject under discussion got up and hastily left the room. That night, my husband said he felt perhaps the boys were getting past the Nanny stage.

For the next few years there were the Mother's Helps. The first two were patients of the local doctor and both were recovering from nervous breakdowns. The doctor seemed to think our home was the ideal place for such patients to rehabilitate themselves — a sort of half-way house between the mental institution and the normal. From all points of view it did the trick and both left to get married.

So the doctor, greatly encouraged by his success, supplied a greater challenge in the person of a reformed alcoholic, although he never actually got around to telling us what her trouble was. She was a wonderful cook and existed quite happily on a permitted daily intake of two pints of brown ale. Sadly, for both of us, no-one had warned me that, as far as she was concerned beer was medicinal, but spirits were lethal. The night when my husband invited two important business contacts and their wives to dinner, she surpassed herself and produced a meal that would have done justice to a French chef. Humble with gratitude, I showed my appreciation by offering her a glass of sherry, as she dished up for the first formal dinner party she had organised for us — and the last!

As we finished the first course, unmistakable strains of grand opera emerged from the kitchen, sung in a clear, sweet treble. They grew louder and less true and suddenly changed to the tune of a war-time march. It was impossible to ignore the sound. One of the wives, a perfect guest, did her best to step elegantly into the breach.

"Your cook obviously enjoys her work," she said sweetly, with her head tilted coyly on one side, "and what a treasure, to be able to produce a soufflé like this." I went to investigate: the "treasure" was lying back in an armchair, clasping a half empty bottle of sherry to her chest and crooning happily. She had succumbed after, all unwittingly, I had whetted her appetite, and had been unable to resist the sherry bottle when she went to the sitting room to clear away our empty glasses while we were at dinner.

"Hello," she said, somewhat aggressively. "Don't look like that, I'll be all right in a minute."

I very much doubted it and set to, to make the gravy.

* * *

Amid all the goings the boys were growing up, and the house was growing bigger: it acquired, not necessarily in chronological order, a cloakroom and a new staircase to make room for it, a large kitchen made by incorporating a coal-house and a larder into the existing kitchen which of course meant a new coal-house and a new larder; a study where, in theory, I should be able to stay at home and write my articles but which faced due south and so became the one room in the house where everyone liked to congregate until we tagged a sun-room on the end of it to lure them out. Somewhere along the line too, there was an extra bedroom and a large spare-bedroom with its own bathroom, all built on pillars because the ground floor was, by then becoming rather unwieldy; a rather splendid porch because the front-door was so draughty, and various bay windows, popped on, here and there, as the easiest way to enlarge the rooms.

It was surprising how easy it became, to slip into the frame of mind where knocking down a wall or cutting in an extra window or two was simplicity itself. It certainly was, we told ourselves, compared to the upheaval and expense of changing houses, which most of our friends seemed to embark on from time to time, as their families grew bigger.

In due course, our friends caught the mood of the place and came up with suggestions for further improvements, some of which proved irresistible. When we adopted any ideas we gave full credit where it was due by calling the latest addition after the person who had suggested it, like "Cotton's Bay" and "Ashton's Loo". Some friends even demonstrated their interest in kind, by leaving a permanent reminder of their visit in the shape of a mural on the kitchen wall or, as in the case of a mosaic artist, a splendid impression of a huge sea-horse made of pebbles from the beach and coloured stones, inset in a rather hideous new red brick outside wall. I chose a sea-horse because I should have liked to adopt it as my family crest on the grounds that it's the only species where the male carries the unborn young in its stomach.

What with one thing and another, the house acquired character, and not always at our instigation; in fact, like some of the most interesting people, it seemed to be "incident prone". It had always, it seems, attracted visitors and when I was quite a youngster, in the Second World War, long before we started pulling its walls about, it did part of its military service as a brothel for the American troops stationed in the area.

It could only have been a very small brothel but, stationed less than four miles from the centre of Norwich it must have been a very busy one for it took years for it to live down its reputation, as I found to my cost: whenever I needed a taxi, I had to school myself to stare some of the older taxi drivers straight in the eye, without flinching at their knowing expression when I told them the address to go to.

One very wintry morning, when my car was out of commission, I ordered a taxi to take me to the station to catch an early train to London. Because the roads were so icy the driver turned up well before the time he'd been ordered, while I was just having a cup of tea. I opened the door to him with the cup in my hand. He was an old man and looked perished with the cold.

"Would you like to come in for a minute and have a warm up?" I said, indicating the cup in my hand. But he never saw it. My question had stirred his memories of the bad old days and frightened out of his wits, he scuttled down the path and into his taxi, almost before I had finished speaking.

He was not the only one who remembered: one afternoon I was resting in bed, convalescing with a slipped disc when two friends arrived to cheer me up. They were a middle-aged married couple whom we had not known for very long although they had lived in the neighbourhood during the war, years before we came to Norfolk.

"This is a very pretty bedroom, dear," said the fussy little wife. "Isn't it, Henry?"

But Henry seemed not to have heard her. He was staring around in a rather bemused way as if he were trying to recall something from another world.

"Henry!" said his wife, summoning him loudly, "don't you think this is an attractive bedroom?"

But Henry was still miles away. He surfaced slowly.

"You know something," he mused, "it's the same but different . . . You know, I have the queerest feeling that, somehow, I've been in this bedroom before."

"You can't have, dear!" his wife consoled him.

But I had a pretty shrewd idea she was wrong!

★ ★ ★

Like the house, we enjoy having visitors, providing that they don't expect us to entertain them, or to pay them a return visit. Neither are we prepared to go out of our way to look after them, except put at their disposal a guest room equipped with every single item that years of travelling around, staying in other people's homes, have taught me, help to make nights spent in unfamiliar surroundings, more bearable. As well as run-of-the-mill commodities like books, biscuits and a radio, there's a well-filled medicine cupboard containing everything from indigestion tablets to paper panties; an electric kettle to fill the hot water bottle, hanging behind the door, or to brew up instant coffee, tea bags or hot lemon, from a selection of jars on the bedside table.

A diet sheet is pinned behind the door to prepare the way for any culinary shortcomings and a notice warning guests to "Keep All Possessions Above Beagle Height." There's also a spare latch-key on an outsize key ring to discourage them from taking it away when they leave and a "Do Not Disturb" notice in five languages, to have outside the bedroom door if they choose to sleep the clock round. And, without ever emerging from the warm cocoon of the pink and white suite, visitors can also catch up with the letter-writing on the reams of note-paper we leave invitingly; experiment with my electric hair-rollers; clean their shoes or mend their socks with the apparatus supplied and meet up with their hosts only when either party has nothing better to do.

We keep the guest room at the ready, with the beds made up for unexpected callers — like the red-haired female radio producer who stayed for a couple of nights while my husband was away. Unfortunately, the second night of her visit, I unexpectedly had to go to London. Even more unexpectedly, my husband returned from his trip in the early hours of the morning and, thinking I was at home and rather than disturb me, he decided to spend what remained of the night in the spare-room. It certainly was a novel way of meeting an attractive redhead for the first time and, I was never really sure if she believed I had not manoeuvred the whole thing.

And for guests suffering from insomnia, there is always the "Visitor's Book," lying invitingly on the bedside table, offering hours of provocative reading and a silent challenge to produce an appropriate entry. Strangely, no-one has ever bettered the very first writing in the book, composed by a gay bachelor after a rather boisterous evening. His poetry was straight from the heart:

"Retire early any guest
Who'd sleep in this fine bed.
No ghost or spirit spoils your rest,
But 'early birds' instead.

A knock upon the wall from Jon,
A shriek from Simon small,
All thoughts of sleep, alas are gone,
From bed you'd better crawl.

So slip up early, friends of mine,
Who value your repose.
Far better be in bed by nine,
The night too soon it goes."

Few people were able to follow his advice, or, unfortunately, his literary standard and it took fifteen years before another visitor, in the shape of a B.B.C. Talks Producer, Paul Humphries, thought to contradict him:

"No bangs woke us.
The birds were muted.
Not even a single owl hooted.
Your visitor, Jean, is
Thus refuted!"

Unfortunately, as the years passed, some of the earlier entries had less light-hearted sequels as we realised the first time an old friend returned with a new wife. We kept the Visitor's Book out of sight because his original entry, composed when he and his first wife were staying with us for another friend's wedding, seemed strangely prophetic:

"The wonderful love of a beautiful girl
And the love of a staunch, true man
And the love of a baby, unafraid,
Have existed since time began.
But the greatest love, the love of
  loves;
Even greater than that of a Mother,
Is the tender and infinite, passionate
  love
Of one drunken chap for another.

— Here's to the next wedding!"

And there was the rather strait-laced parent who demanded to be told just what his twelve-year-old son had been up to, when he had stayed with us and written in the book a few months earlier,

"Thanks for eight days of debauchery and the BAD life."

As far as I could remember we had allowed him to sit up until midnight, watching television and drink half-a-pint of beer every evening. But, afterwards, we scribbled across the fly leaf of the book "Nothing in this book shall be used as evidence . . . "

According to the book, there was also plenty of evidence of shortcomings in the plumbing system: why did such crises always occur at the weekend, just as, why was Sunday the day we invariably ran out of bathroom stationery? As a result of the weekend crisis, our cesspool earned itself an unfair share of literary immortality.

Once upon a time, that down-to-earth institution, buried deep in the bottom of our garden was quite exemplary.

It functioned efficiently and quietly, unobtrusively aided by a discreet visit from the appropriate authority to empty it once a year, usually in the darkness of a winter's afternoon. But with the advent of detergents and the building of many new houses in the area, all with washing machines and waste disposal units, the cesspool demanded to be emptied every month.

It became a costly business. It was even more annoying because, true to form, my super efficient neighbour whose washing was always out on the line on Monday morning, a good two hours before mine and whose children never had the slightest difficulty in passing their exams, had a cesspool which by sheer good fortune, was sited over a seam of sand and therefore never appeared to need emptying. The fact that my clay soil was so good for the roses was little compensation for giving my neighbour, once a month, justification for turning up her nose on our account.

There was the Bank Holiday weekend when, with a house-full of guests the cesspool, with uncanny timing, overflowed into every drain in the house. I telephoned the sanitary department who could only offer to send a plumber to "tide me over" until the emptying van could go into action after the holiday. He was a splendid plumber: he prodded and poked at all the drains and inspection chambers and outlets until the level of water subsided a little.

"Reckon it'll larst you a couple of days, 'till they clear you out nice and proper like," he said, scratching his head, adding as an after-thought;

"Till they do, I reckon you'd be well advised to hold your water."

Of course, the weekend was suitably recorded, with a dire warning, in the Visitor's Book

"Hold your water
Darling daughter!
Something that you never oughter."

As the entries in the Book increased and the house grew, it became increasingly obvious that, as far as the boys were concerned, despite my super-human efforts to run a normal home, keep up with a career and give my sons a fair share of attention, sooner or later, one of those commitments was bound to suffer and my husband decreed that the time had come to protect his sons by sending them to boarding school. It had always been his intention to send them and I had been equally determined that they should stay at home. The argument that my work was increasingly time-consuming only strengthened my husband's argument plus the fact that he had recently become suspicious that his eldest son, at least, had inherited the true journalist's enthusiasm for a good 'stunt': his latest exploit was original enough to develop into a story for any boy's magazine.

He and a friend, who were both rapidly becoming aware of the charms of the opposite sex, had spent an afternoon when they should have been watching a school rugger match, in the grounds of the local girl's school, armed with buckets and a long ladder, masquerading as window cleaners. They wore jeans and old shirts and walked about completely unchallenged, peering through the windows until they found the class-room where the objects of their interest were having their lesson. There they polished the window and grimaced to the admiring girls, behind the teacher, to their hearts' content. When we heard of this exploit, through the mother of one of the girls, I too was lost in admiration and suspected my husband's irrational disapproval was largely because his son had chosen to spend the afternoon doing this rather than watch a game of rugger. I prayed that boarding school would not spoil his initiative.

It didn't, although the very next term we deposited him at the gates of one of the great British public schools, purported to have reared men who built the Empire on which the sun never sets. Perhaps the fact that the sun rarely seemed to put in an appearance in this isolated Midland village, where for nine months of the year a wind whipped down the main street, straight from the Urals, had something to do with the strength of character of those who spent their formative years there.

"This place could look pretty bleak!" commented my son with the carefully-controlled casualness bred during eight years in an English Prep. School. It was the understatement of his thirteen years. The grey, stone buildings looming up like a gaol, on either side of the deserted village street, were unfamiliar and forbidding in the mocking warmth of the late September evening. It was not only the end of summer, it was the end of an epoch.

"Dear God," I thought, as I prepared to abandon him. "How could it look bleaker than it does at this moment, this out-of-the-way prison where we had sentenced him for five years?"

"When those five years have passed," I thought to myself, "I shall be quite old. When he comes home again, for good, it will be useless for me to keep pulling out my white hairs, there will be far too many. And probably, by that time I shan't even care."

On the one hundred mile car journey home I suddenly realised that it was more than likely that he would never come home again for good. To my husband's disgust, because at that point he had just decided to stop for a meal, I burst into tears and howled like a baby for the rest of the journey.

When five years had passed, I was still pulling out the white hairs. I could look back on five pretentious Speech Days when I wore a succession of inconspicuous hats, chosen with far more care and trepidation than any Ascot ones: I recalled ten deliriously hectic school holidays and four long, lazy, summer ones, that ambled gently along.

The holidays long or short, all followed a similar pattern: they started with a rather strained first meal at home, followed by a gradual process of unwinding until, after twenty-four hours had passed, it seemed as if the Boarding School-Boy had never been away. Except that never again, for the rest of his life, did I take his presence for granted. Near the end of every holiday came the inevitable re-winding, evidenced by a lack of communication for two or three days, as if he were deliberately withdrawing from his family, severing his home ties and schooling himself to prepare for the new term. Or was it I who was tensing up at the prospect of his departure?

I could look back too, on exhausting exeat weekends when, like a family of refugees, we huddled in the corners of unfriendly hotels, with their shilling-in-the-slot gas fires and no bedside lights and where we dare not utter a word of complaint about the soggy cabbage or poor service, for fear of being struck off the register in an area where every hotel, for miles around, was booked up at exeat weekends for months, and even years ahead.

How those weekends taxed our ingenuity, as well as our digestion! Saturdays were easy: there was an eager get-together lunch, followed by a cricket or rugger match to watch in the afternoon; then an enormous high tea and perhaps a School play, or a concert in the evening. But on Sundays, it was a matter of contriving to fill in the time between three enormous meals and, as the hour for departure approached, our son's complexion usually acquired a definite greenish tinge. I never managed to discover whether this was due to the incredible amount of food he had consumed or to the strain of imminent separation, even 'though, during his second term, he vomited at five o'clock on Sunday afternoon, on three consecutive exeats.

In the summer terms, Sundays were somewhat easier: there were plenty of local stately homes to visit and dozens of private gardens, mercifully open in aid of charity. After a couple of years, we discovered a stretch of river where we could hire a small motor-boat for the day. The sun shone, it seemed, all that summer.

Public schools are usually sited in the most isolated parts of the country no doubt for excellent reasons, but, in these days of better parent-teacher collaboration, it is surely time for the schools to consider the parents' welfare a little, by including, for instance, a printed list of local amenities, along with the clothes lists, tuck shop accounts and notices of forthcoming increases in the school fees. It took me two sons and some five years' hard-work, to discover such possibilities as two cinemas open on Sunday afternoon, a bowling alley and a museum, all within a twenty mile radius. We eventually also found a golf course, prepared to accept Sunday members, and a disused airfield where the boys could learn to drive the car. A go-cart club proved a top attraction for a while and so did a sailing club, on a local gravel pit where a handy crew was always welcome. But such potential delights, which would have been such a godsend during the first rather demanding terms, took a lot of finding and only really benefitted the second son by helping him to enjoy rather than endure his exeats.

Whatever a British Public School did to build my sons' characters, as a parent, the first five years getting to know it, certainly strengthened my own character. If I had had a daughter, much as I would have wanted to send her to my isolated almer mater, I could never have faced those exeats. I would rather have settled for a rival establishment, sited within striking distance of a luxury hotel, where guests were still a major consideration and where there were good shops and a thriving theatre.

On the other hand for a parent whose sons were at boarding school, there were compensations. I felt entitled to bow out, gracefully, from the role of disciplinarian and stop worrying in the holidays about whether my sons were spending too much time watching television, going to the cinema or chasing the girls. Discipline was the school's responsibility and, if during the remaining one-third of the year, the boys tried to make up for lost time, I could not blame them, or spoil their fun by telling them it was long past their bedtime.

Now and again, I had certain qualms about just how much discipline they were receiving during the all-important two-thirds of their life, but I managed to suppress these maternal misgivings engendered, for instance, when, on the first day of his very first holiday, the heir-apparent boasted, unashamedly, that he had succeeded in going right through the term without a bath, a feat which was born out by the condition of his detachable stiff white collars. He also dropped hints about hair-raising happenings concerning a certain "Wag Trent" who kept an illicit motor-bike at school, and about a sixteen-year old American exchange scholar who took a girl to Paris for the weekend and was expelled for his one-upmanship. So was the aspiring schoolboy journalist who leaked, to a Sunday newspaper, the story of the never-to-be-repeated junior school outing to Whipsnade Zoo, which started with beer and rowdyism on the train, and culminated in an unfortunate incident involving the hind quarters of an elephant and a broken beer bottle. But, at the same time, mingled with the misgivings, was relief that such escapades were a good deal healthier than my major twin fears; drugs and homosexuality. There was consolation too, in believing that, in the end, any school which had to cope with all those happenings, in a single term, should be able to enforce the amount of discipline required by a fairly amenable thirteen-year-old. My own most immediate problem therefore, was whether to make him his favourite chocolate mousse for lunch, three days running.

* * *

Before the boys went away to boarding school, it had reached the stage that, in trying to combine motherhood and a career, holidays apart, the only time I devoted the whole of one day to the children was on the very few occasions when they were ill in bed. Then, whatever might have been my personal commitments, I would go to enormous lengths to cancel my arrangements so as to leave myself quite free to hover round my son's bedside, doing all those rather superficial little tasks that I thought, they thought, were the responsibility of a truly devoted mother. At such times, I felt I was REALLY NEEDED and responded with a will, smothering the patients with attention, in compensation for all those other times I had not been around to console them, when they might have liked me to be.

I cooked tempting little dishes, which they struggled, manfully, to eat, but which invariably proved far too sickly; and I fussed around the sick-room, filling it with comics and grapes, iced drinks and a television set, flowered sheets and boiled sweets, until it looked the boudoir of some neurotic princeling. No wonder its occupant's convalescence was often unduly prolonged!

Unfortunately for them, however, invalid or infant cooking, like most other maternal skills, was something I had learned the hard way, as far as they were concerned so that, even today, the very mention of "Barley Kernel Pudding" fills me with shame and remorse. It represents the culmination of my domestic shortcomings, compounded from a combination of ignorance, over-conscientiousness, lack of common-sense and a slavish devotion to the printed word.

It happened because "Barley Kernel Pudding" figured prominently in the current infant diet sheet I was following. It was referred to over and over again as the ideal ingredient in a newly-weaned infant's menu. Still smarting from the scathing letter I had recently received from a firm of baby food manufacturers, warning me about distending my three-month's-old son's stomach after I had enquired why his appetite was not appeased by one-and-a-half feeding bottles full of their milk mixture at each meal, I was taking no more nutritional chances and missing out on something like "Barley Kernels" which might well possess some unspecified properties, quite vital to an infant's well being. The determination to use them increased on discovering that, either because they were obsolete or highly desirable, they were quite unobtainable in the shops, in post-war Britain.

No-one strangely enough, seemed quite certain just what they were, which, as the diet had been compounded by an American paedetrician, was not entirely surprising. Until, one day, when I had almost given up hope of tracing the elusive elixir, an elderly neighbour remembered using it for making milk puddings for her own family, and thought she might still have some left, in a tin on her pantry shelf.

Sure enough, she had and triumphantly, every third day, I used half-an-ounce to make a milk pudding for my ever-hungry first born. It looked an unspectacular concoction, hardly worth-while making so much fuss about — unless the fat, rice-like grains, floating about in the milk, really did contain some special cordial. One day, spooning mouthfuls of the stuff into my long-suffering offspring, in a particularly bright light, I studied the granules particularly closely; it didn't need a magnifying glass, or more than my limited culinary ability, to see that they were maggots.

For some reason, however, I never seemed to react in a particularly conscientious way when my husband retired to his sick-bed. Maybe, this was because he made it so patently obvious that he felt it was part of his marital right to have a fussing, solicitous wife, hovering over him, smoothing his fevered brow and straightening his sheets with the prim devotion of a hospital probationer. His groans, whenever his temperature rose above 99.9 could be heard in the adjoining room, and were audible reminders of my loving duty, despite his perpetual request, to be left alone in his suffering.

The groans were just too heart-rending, so I left him alone, with only the mildest feeling of guilt and, after making sure that he had his medicines and his comforts at hand, thankfully escaped about my business, salving my conscience by telephoning him, at intervals during the day, to reassure myself that he still had enough strength to groan.

There was one particular occasion however, when this treatment badly misfired. It happened because I was committed to go up to London for a radio broadcast on the day when my husband had arranged a dentist appointment, in Norwich, to have a tooth out by a local anaesthetic. As a man who had the strongest aversion to injections, he would much preferred to have let the dentist pull the tooth without giving him one. But modern dentists don't seem to work like that!

Just before the time for my broadcast, the old, familiar feeling of wifely solicitousness caught up with me. It could hardly have been a more inconvenient moment but I could not quite manage to suppress it so, with just ten minutes to go before the live transmission, I reached for the telephone and dialled my home.

A very bruised and barely audible voice answered the telephone. It's owner was in agony; but AGONY. Aspirins? He'd taken near-lethal doses of the strongest pain-killers. Nothing was having the slightest effect. He could hardly hold his head up. He would just make a brave attempt to listen to my broadcast and he would then crawl straight upstairs to bed.

Waves of guilt washed over me; a female Nero, fiddling while Rome burned. But surely this was getting the whole thing out of perspective? I stopped indulging and steeled myself to get a mental grip and concentrate on the imminent broadcast. After all, no-one had actually died from having a tooth out! Or had they? It was two hours later, standing at the railway station, waiting for the train home, that I seemed to remember hearing about a man who had died, from just that.

I dashed to a telephone and dialled our number: there was no reply. I telephoned his office: his secretary said he was having the afternoon off. I telephoned him again: no reply. By this time, I could visualise him, lying helpless within arm's reach of the bedside telephone, unconscious or too weak from loss of blood or some mysterious reaction to the injection, to stretch out his hand and lift the receiver. I telephoned his office again: too late. The only reply was the firm's answering machine. I telephoned a friend: there was no reply.

By this time, there was just three minutes to go before my train left. Three minutes in which to atone for putting my own career before the well-being of my long-suffering husband. Three minutes to accept responsibility for a life-time of irresponsibility. Memories, from my reporter's days, flooded back, of all the inquests where a victim's family might have averted tragedy by taking positive action. I had three minutes, if it were not already too late, to take some positive action. I took the only kind I could think of: I dialled the police!

Somehow, there was a grain of comfort, on the endless two-hour train journey home, in the thought that, when it came to a real emergency, I had not shirked my responsibility. On the contrary, I had faced up to the worst possible implications of the situation and acted. Maybe, there was such a thing as womanly intuition, after all, which God forbid, might more than justify my action. By the time the train drew into its destination I was almost buoyant with self-righteousness.

For the whole length of the platform, I felt slightly inebriated. Then I saw the notice chalked up on the message board, by the ticket collector: I read my name and the instruction to report to the Station Master's Office. My shaking legs hardly carried me there. Two mobile police, with kind, sympathetic faces, were waiting for me.

"We've come to prepare you," they said and I sat down on a convenient chair. "We thought we should just warn you that your husband's in a fiendish temper."

Who said the British police were not the best in the world?

These two obviously thought they had crashed in on the first stage of a divorce case: I learned that, in response to the emergency call, they had gone to the house, got no reply to the bell or their knocks and bangs on the front door, so had forced their way in through a

Portrait of the Author
by Edward Seago.

My Mother – before housework took its toll.

A large, very sprawling and rather ungracious family home.

Peter Le-Britton.

A permanent reminder of a friend's visit – the only species where the male carries the unborn young.

Bangaline Lionel's Legatee – the troublesome beagle who just grew handsome. *Peter Le-Britton.*

Taffy.

Dear Yvonne

I am thrilled that you're going to tell me a few home truths. Hope it's not too much of a shock to me

yours

Sara Harrison.

Handwriting of
"a dedicated career girl".

Seafarer.

The Home Fleet.

The "sardine tin" in Majorca

and *The Enterprise,* part of "The Man's World".

window. On the upstairs landing they met my husband emerging from the bedroom to see what all the noise was about.

"You should have heard the language," they said, in reluctant admiration, "when we explained we'd come because of his wife's emergency call. Said he'd always known he was married to a mad woman. Now she wouldn't even let him switch the telephone off, to get an afternoon's rest, without becoming hysterical."

"I'm not the least hysterical," I protested.

"No," one of them agreed, understandingly, "but all the same, I shouldn't be in too much of a hurry to get home, if I were you."

★ ★ ★

On the rare occasions when I was ill in bed, it was quite another story: the telephone was a life-line through which, even in near-delirium, I struggled to maintain contact with the outside world to ensure that life continued to run as smoothly as possible for the other members of the family. They on their part, tended to reciprocate my interest, by congregating in the bedroom, whenever they had nothing better to do, cheering me up, they thought, with loud cross-talk and banter.

The time I had the chicken-pox, for instance. I lay back on the pillows, feeling unbelievably wretched while my six-year-old read to me aloud, slowly and laboriously:

"The cat sat on the mat. The mat was red . . . "

He looked up and contemplated me.

"So is your face," he said, with a grin of admiration. "It's all red freckles. Coo!" he murmured, delightfully, "I don't think you've room for another freckle anywhere."

"Just go on reading," I murmured weakly, concentrating on trying to find some sort of satisfaction from the halting intonement that "The cat was not red . . . ", for, in a manner of speaking, this was the one tangible justification for his rather chequered first year's schooling. In that case it should help to counter-balance the final achievement of his year — giving me chicken-pox on the first day of the summer holidays.

In my near-lightheadedness I assembled a mental balance sheet of the achievements and set-backs of his first school year: these stumbling sentences of his were the ultimate consolation for the anguish of that day nine months ago when I surrendered him to another authority for the first time in his life. I remembered coaxing him up the long drive to the seat of learning: he was green with fright and dwarfed by his unfamiliar grey, flannel suit which made him look as if he were wearing fancy dress. He managed not to cry. But I was not so stoic when I got back to a home unbelievably quiet and empty without him.

But he was not away from the home for very long: a continuous series of colds and bilious attacks and unexplained temperatures kept him in bed almost as much as he was at school.

"It's always the same, their first term; it's the strain; they seem to catch everything that's going," the experienced mothers assured me.

The second term started more aggressively, with the loss of his front tooth, in a fight with another boy.

"He's just finding his feet," said his proud father and started taking a keener interest in his son's activities. His timing was unfortunate. Mumps was the thing going at that moment. His son was just hatching an attack and, in accordance with the new-found partnership, he shared his affliction with his father.

"Far better to get these things over young," muttered the doctor, with a quizzical look at my husband, confined to bed for fear of the sinister complications which sometimes affects the mature male mumps victims. My son, apparently overhearing the doctor's advice, obliged by starting whooping cough and passing it on to the baby, who gave it to his grandmother.

Once the long winter and spring was over, we hoped for better things.

"Chicken-pox is nothing," said the doctor, confirming my diagnosis of the blistery spots on my son's arm, "It needn't even keep him in bed," It didn't. It just kept me there.

And that was how I came to be lying, shivering, under mountains of bedclothes, on the hottest day of the summer, listening to my first-born intoning about the cat who sat on the mat. I certainly wished that I had "got it over young" and that my husband had too. I remembered how I had nursed him through scarlet fever, as well as mumps, at the same time as his son had these complaints and while I was consoling my mother who was "whooping it up" and I reckoned that, on balance, our son's illness-ridden first year at school had been something of an achievement — socially, if not scholastically.

* * *

One of the many social difficulties a working wife must learn to contend with, is to make time to share her husband's leisure interests, when he so desires, as well as trying to pursue her own. Ironically, husbands of non-domestic women seem particularly sensitive on this score and most eager that their wife should spend her hard-earned leisure in companionable togetherness, however uncomfortable or inconvenient.

So on most Saturday afternoons, during the winter, after a hectic week's work and with a hundred-and-one jobs waiting to be done around the house, I could be found shivering on the touchline of some windswept rugger ground, huddled with other loyal wives, watching our husbands writhing about in the mud with the abandon of overgrown school-boys.

"I shouldn't like to have to wash their clothes," murmured an impartial spectator, standing beside me at a particularly muddy game. How right she was I know to my cost but, as a rugger wife, that was the least of my grievances.

Golfer's wives who are sportingly inclined, can always take up the game and turn it into an active shared interest, although this sport is far too time consuming for a working wife to hope to play with any degree of proficiency. The wives of tennis or sailing enthusiasts are on to a far better thing, while a cricketer's wife can hardly complain at having to relax in a deck-chair on a summer's afternoon and admire her husband in his immaculate white flannels. This is the most soothing pastime I know and even if the better-half is out for a duck, a cricketer is too good a sportsman to vent his spleen on his wife and he will spend the rest of his team's innings, sitting beside her in companionable if disgruntled togetherness.

However, there is not the slightest hope of the rugby wife being able to relax, even if she were warm enough. From half-time she will be needed in the clubhouse, to cut rounds of sandwiches for teams of hungry men, few of whom will have eaten much before the game. She must then wait patiently while they wolf the sandwiches, wash them down with endless pints of beer and chant the songs to remind them of their virile young manhood.

Rugby players expect their wives not only to tolerate but also to share their enthusiasm for the big love of their lives, a game which certainly doesn't end with the final whistle. There were the dances on Saturday evenings when, after a hard game in the afternoon, my husband could hardly hobble round the floor: there were visits to the cinema when he would leap up at a crucial moment in the film and stand rigid, quite helpless and unable to move an inch, with cramp in his leg muscles, while I tried to placate the people sitting behind.

Perhaps it was something of an omen that on the very day we became officially engaged, he split his lip during the game and had three stitches put into it which effectively severed that zone of communication, for several weeks.

"Just an occupational hazard. You'll have to get used to that sort of thing," consoled an experienced friend who had watched her own husband carried unconscious off the field at Twickenham, during an International two days before their daughter was born.

Twickenham, of course, is the Mecca of the rugby world. On my tri-annual pilgrimages, I endured bleak picnics on draughty car parks, where a flask of whisky was a medical necessity. Muffled under layers of warm clothing and with one's face turning red, white and blue with cold, it was never easy to look one's best and as each year passed, I wondered whether it was just the cold or the inevitable passage of time that had so ravaged my contemporaries, since we had last met at Wimbledon some six months earlier.

There was one particular England-Wales match when I determined to put a good face on for the occasion: I sported a jaunty red ski cap with a peak that shielded the top half of my face and a scarlet scarf that covered the other half. I had scarlet gloves to match and thought the whole effect was rather good. My husband stared, rather proudly, I fancied, when he saw me. Then his face clouded with horror.

"You can't go in that outfit," he roared. "red's the Welsh colours."

Even in foreign parts there was no guarantee against the influence of the oval ball: it was a glorious Sunday in spring when I first saw Rome. The sun shone from the Italian blue sky and the handsome young Roman rugger-playing friend of my husband, who met us off the plane, looked like a worthy descendant of the gladiators of old. As we purred along the banks of the Tiber, in his sleek sports car, I studied his classical profile and elegant black hair and thought that here, at last, was a fringe benefit of the game.

"What a shame it's not a Saturday so that we could have seen a game of rugby," I remarked, conversationally.

My husband guffawed, from the back seat.

Eureka! Rugby was played on Sundays in Rome and we were on our way to be made honorary members of Rugby Roma and watch this modern Archimedes lead his team to victory.

As a rugby widow of many year's standing, I feel that any foolish spinsters who gravitate towards rugby pavilions on Saturday afternoons should be warned in advance as to the respective position of the game and marriage, as symbolised by a girl friend whose Saturday wedding ceremony was nicely timed to allow her and the groom to dash to the rugger ground, after the reception. While the bride, in her going-away outfit, watched from the pavilion, her new husband, possibly because he was so primed with champagne, played the game of a life-time. This case was certainly an exception: few rugger players would even consider getting married until the season was over, unless, like my friend, an English scrum-half, Simon Clarke, they managed to persuade the bride to go on tour with their club team, as a honeymoon.

Not even the close of the playing season signifies a complete recession. Indeed, I found this was the time when a really loyal wife could come into her own and literally, take over the field, for children's sports days or fetes in aid of club funds. And there was one memorable summer's afternoon when our club arranged a stone-picking picnic for women and children, in a diabolic attempt to improve the surface of a new pitch.

As for seeking consolation in the hope that, after all, rugger is only a young man's game. This discounts the most important man on the field, the Referee, a position that should be the ultimate end of all good players to ensure that, like Field Marshals, they need never retire. Moreover, a good referee not only requires an even keener knowledge of the rules than any player, but must also be able to keep up, physically, with the fastest back on the field, a feat which, as the years roll on, takes an increasing toll of the wife: she will not only have to be a dab hand at applying the embrocation, but also deputise for her exhausted husband with weekend chores like walking the dog or getting the coal in.

With it all, I have, nevertheless, often wished that, along with the crash course I took on mothercraft and the evening classes I went to, to learn to cook on a primus stove, I had managed to fit in a course of lectures on the theory of rugby, to enable me to take a more intelligent interest in the game and shout pertinent comments from the touchline, to win approving glances from every male within earshot.

Would I have had this part of my life different? I certainly thought so, until the day when my elder son, aged ten, came home from school with his hand red and swollen.

"I've broken my thumb at rugger," he announced, rather apologetically.

"Oh, goodness!" I said, "your father will be pleased." With a shock, I realised, quite ridiculously, that I was too!

3

Working at Holidays

THE Family Holiday is one of the institutions a working mother should fight to preserve at all costs, particularly when her children are away at boarding school: it is one of the few occasions when all members of the family can get to know each other again after a term's separation, keep in touch with newly-formed interests and, above all, make sure that they can still communicate — even if they heartily disagree.

To this end *Seafarer* was a godsend. She was a sturdy old motor cruiser, sharp at each end, converted from an ex-German ship's life-boat from the First World War. She was twenty-six foot long and had been fitted with a saloon, galley and tiny for'ard cabin. With her four bunk beds and painted pale blue and white inside and marine blue and white outside, she was a nautical home to satisfy the most demanding embryonic jack tar. Moreover, her old-fashioned wheel and chain gear that had to be cranked vigorously as soon as the temperamental old engine was coaxed into action, ensured that manoeuvring her was no job for a weekend sailor.

Despite her name, there was never any question of taking her to sea: her shallow draught and generous super-structure would have ensured an uncomfortable coastal trip in the best of weathers but, for the Norfolk Broads she was a perfect craft: low enough, with her mini mast down, to slip under all the bridges and stalwart enough to ride at anchor in the middle of Barton Broad in any wind, acting as mother ship to half-a-dozen flimsy dinghies whose owners had tied up alongside and come aboard.

Moreover, it was understood from the beginning, that *Seafarer* was a man's world. I was welcome to go along but, in terms of responsibility, it was all theirs. In fact, I should hardly be expected to lift a finger to help. In theory this sounded the perfect arrangement.

In practice it never quite worked out that way: but, as I stood in the tiny galley, hour after hour, in the heat of most summer Sunday afternoons, washing up an endless assortment of dirty mugs in a tiny bowl of cold water while my menfolk welcomed a continuous stream of visitors aboard for hot soup, tea or coffee, I perspired in a warm glow of family togetherness.

Anyhow, where housekeeping was concerned, there could have been no better training ground for the boys than the tiny galley, some four feet square, where they could produce a meal on two burners and learn the hard way that plastic dinner plates don't respond well to being warmed up in the oven and that a calor gas stove is something to be treated with the utmost respect. No-one who lives near the Norfolk Broads can remain unaware of the dreadful toll of explosions which, more often than not, are caused by a build-up of gas in the boat, from a fire or cooker. But, even though we installed a safety routine for using the gas, we too once came unfortunately near to blowing up.

It happened one summer's day when *Seafarer* was moored on the banks of the River Ant and we were eating lunch in the shelter of her roomy well. Two friends were with us, a young married couple who lived abroad, and revelled in the peace and quiet of this picture-book English scene: but not for long.

They were just the sort of visitors we liked because the man, without even being asked, cleared away after the meal, piled up the dirty plates on the draining board in the galley, and with superb efficiency, stood the used cutlery upright to soak, in an empty pan of water on the cooker, then he put the kettle on for coffee. The rest of us just lay and sunbathed in the well, at the other end of the boat. The paragon of a visitor joined us there while he waited for the kettle to boil to make the coffee.

"Kettle's boiling," I murmured encouragingly, after a few minutes, as I heard it whistle.

He took the hint and disappeared through the hatch. A second later he announced, rather portentously from the galley, "We're on fire."

It was said in such a matter of fact tone, it sounded like a rather poor joke: no-one moved, until suddenly, something made me stir myself to call his bluff and go and investigate. There was nothing matter of fact about my shrieks which brought the whole ship's complement to their feet.

The fearsome sight that greeted them was a saucepan full of flames burning merrily, almost to ceiling height, caused by the bone handles of the knives catching fire from the light under the adjoining kettle. But after the first moment of panic I was almost calmness itself.

While the men watched, spell-bound, I seized the knives, one at a time, by their blades and, like a torch-thrower in a circus, hurled them, with magnificent precision, through the tiny porthole. The first four knives went through perfectly and I was almost enjoying it. But success went to my head and the fifth was a bad shot: the knife just missed the porthole and, still flaming, clattered down a gap between the hull and the draining board which, presumably, led straight down into the bilge of the boat where there were usually plenty of traces of oil and petrol.

"Abandon ship," yelled my husband, and taking command he seized the saucepan and its last flickering knives, rushed through the cabin with it and leapt ashore. Stuffing my burnt hand in my pocket, I followed obediently, marvelling at the presence of mind with which on the way he also remembered to collect the fire extinguisher fixed importantly to the side of the wheel house; a splendid gesture this, until he discovered that the instructions embossed on its side were too small to read without his spectacles and he had left those in the cabin.

Undeterred, and with the spirit of Drake coursing through his veins, he banged the top of the fire extinguisher and, aiming its nozzle through the porthole, pumped vigorously, directing a thin dribble of sauce-like foam vaguely towards the gap behind the back of the sink, into the bilge. Nothing happened except the foam ran out. After a suitable interval, during which the boat failed to explode, I rather sheepishly collected the handleless knives from the bank and we all re-embarked.

The visitors, tactfully, started doing the washing up. Even more tactfully, a few days after they had left, we received, as a present from them, a most fitting memento of their visit in the shape of a box of six stainless steel knives with the name *Seafarer* engraved, with dignified respect, on each of the handles.

The old boat certainly warranted our respect for as well as teaching the boys domestic skills, she afforded them some valuable lessons in seamanship: there was the day in late October when, after a week of incessant rain, it was time to move her from her summer mooring on Barton Broad and sail down the winding River Ant, back to the boatyard where she always spent the winter.

The last trip of the year was always a nostalgic one, marking the passing of yet another summer and this time, my ten-year old clamoured to be allowed to take a turn at the helm. Why are there no age limits or L plates or the equivalent of driving tests for helmsmen? Without them it would have been unreasonable to refuse.

Bursting with importance, our younger was given command. He took up his position on an orange box and, heady with the sight of the deserted wintry-looking Broad and the power of the pulsating engine, he opened the throttle and we swept across the wide expanse of water, the wash swelling in spray behind us, speeding with a verve that caused *Seafarer's* old timbers to creak in joyful echo of her young life-boat days when she hastened to the rescue of those in distress. I glanced apprehensively at my husband but, as usual at such moments, he ignored what he chose to consider unreasonable caution.

We were across the Broad in no time and even when it narrowed into the river we hardly slackened speed: but here, the river was so swollen by all the rain, that there seemed much more room than usual to manoeuvre. Round the first bend we swung with the little tender bucking and bouncing like a mad thing behind us. Then Simon did deign to throttle back the engine, but not soon enough to be able to make quite sure of his bearings. At the next bend, we seemed well clear of the bank. Suddenly there was a grinding crash as if the engine had either seized up or gone into reverse, the boat lurched sickeningly and slewed broadside across the river. My husband leapt into action, cut the engine, seized the wheel and gradually steadied the boat down. It didn't take much investigation to find the two foot gash in her hull, just below the water line, which had penetrated through two of her three skins. Eventually, we discovered it had been made by a submerged steel pile, marking what normally would have been the bank of the river.

Meanwhile, the immediate concern was to stop up the gap in the boat where water was pouring into the bilge. We pushed pillows and rugs against it and kept up a non-stop pumping operation, turn and turn about, on the little hand pump, but it was soon obvious that it was a losing battle. Buckets and basins were brought into action but, in no time, the first sinister trickle of water seeped through the floor boards. I, tentatively, suggested it was perhaps time to abandon ship — but no-one appeared to hear.

Instead, everyone seemed to be hanging on the words of the white-faced cause of the trouble who, until now, had professed to know the river like the back of his hand and, even 'though proved wrong, was re-instating himself into favour by announcing importantly that he was pretty certain there was a sand-bank in the river, about two hundred yards downstream.

The significance of this eluded me, but my husband, wearing the expression of a captain, either intent on saving his ship or going down with it on the bridge, re-started the engine, took the helm and gently eased his heavily-listing command forward, roaring to the rest of us to "keep pumping". While the boys obeyed, I took off my shoes and socks in order to be ready to swim to safety at any moment and then, paddling about, ankle deep in icy water, stowed some of our more valuable possessions, like the radio and a bottle of whisky, into a hold-all.

When the water was on average about three inches above the floor boards, a gentle grinding under the keel announced that we had found the sandbank and touched down, fortunately just about six feet away from the river bank, just near enough to hurl ashore everything that could be removed from the boat; mattresses, sleeping bags, spare clothes, cushions, the lot: it was an undignified exodus and no self-respecting life-boat should have been subjected to such ignominy.

My hold-all full of personal salvage went with us in the dinghy. Safe on the river bank we watched, helplessly, as *Seafarer* listed agonisingly to starboard and then, in a final death rigor, jerked onto her side and settled with her deck just clear of the water. It seemed the end of an epoch. Silently and reverently we turned away — and walked across the fields in search of a house and telephone.

But as it turned out, she was made of sterner stuff than we dared hope. The boatyard sealed her up and pumped her out and she was repaired and dry within a fortnight. After a good winter's rest, she was out and about the next summer, none the worse for the experience and eager for new adventures.

Such is the accepted male supremacy aboard ship that only, in the most dire extremity, was it ever suggested, that I should take the helm — to leave the men free to cope with other problems, as happened, for instance, on the way to the tennis party. It was my elder son who had been invited. He and I were spending the weekend on *Seafarer* and the party was being held at a house a few miles down the river. The opportunity of creating an impression by stepping off the boat in his immaculate white flannels, before a group of admiring guests, was something his young male ego could hardly resist.

On the face of it there was nothing to it although it did take most of the morning to travel by water the few miles that, in a car, would have taken less than twenty minutes. We moored for an early lunch, within about half-an-hour of our destination and while I, relenting for once about my rule of non-participation in boating chores, fried up eggs and sausage, he got himself ready for the party.

It had been a showery morning. We kept the canvas canopy up over the well of the boat and ate our lunch inside the saloon where, once he had gone off, I planned to settle down and spend the afternoon catching up on my writing. After lunch we set off on the final stretch of the journey, to the inevitable noisy accompaniment of music from his transistor. The clouds cleared, the sun came out and it looked all set for an idyllic summer afternoon.

"Will you just take the helm for a bit while I get the canopy down?" he yelled from the well, as I cleared away the lunch things.

"Won't it wait until we get there?"

"We're running a bit late," he said. "No time then."

He throttled back the engine to its minimum, cutting our speed, surrendered the wheel to me and scrambled through a flap in the canvas hood, outside onto the stern of the boat to undo the back clips. It was quite a tricky operation to get the hood down, single handed, at any time, let alone when the boat was moving.

A speed boat flipped past, their radio

even noiser than ours and we swayed uncomfortably as we caught their wash. The occupants waved apologetically. I corrected our course impeccably and waved back. Round the next bend in the river I could just see our destination. I called to Jonathan: he was making a long job of the canopy. I called again and there was no reply so I stuck my head through the flap in the canopy and called again. From somewhere in the far distance, a long way behind, it seemed, there came a faint answering cry: but my son was nowhere to be seen.

I panicked: I leaned far out to try and see where the voice was coming from, but there was no-one in sight.

"Jonathan!" I yelled, at the top of my voice.

"Here," came an indignant roar.

"Where?" I shrieked insanely. Then I saw him: far behind me, behind the boat and behind the dinghy trailing behind that, just emerging from the waters I could see the head and shoulders of my first born being dragged through the water as he hung on to the back of the dinghy, for dear life.

"The engine: cut the engine," he yelled, mustering all his fading strength after at least ten minutes in the water, as *Seafarer* went gently up the bank.

His arrival at the tennis party couldn't have been more memorable.

★ ★ ★

Eventually, as far as family holidays were concerned, the time came to venture further afield and I dreamt of spending three hard-earned weeks of complete leisure lying prone on some sun-drenched Mediterranean beach, soaking up the sun and turning an enviable shade of brown and with nothing more arduous to worry about then whether there was time for another little dip to cool off, before the next Campari?

But in a nautically-minded family, it was inconceivable that we should be anywhere near an expanse of water without having a boat to mess about in; if not a cruiser, at least a dinghy or speed-boat for water ski-ing and exploring a new coast-line. Hiring a boat, for any length of time was, with the shortage of foreign currency, out of the question, so the alternative was to take our own — towing it behind the car for the simple, bumper-to-bumper, eight hundred or so mile journey to the South of France or Sunny Spain, in the peak of the holiday season. According to my adventurous husband it would make "an exciting start to the holiday" but, after the first couple of such temper-fraying expeditions, he decided there must be an easier way of getting to our chosen destination. He came to this conclusion the year the back axle on the boat trailer snapped, on one of the busiest stretches of continental auto-route and a wheel detached itself and spun across the road and disappeared into a French river, never to be seen again.

The traffic jam, caused by this diversion, was impressive in any language and, some six hours later, we had the dubious honour of arriving in Fréjus with a motor-cycle escort of French police, anxious to ensure that the improvised repair to the axle caused no further disaster and we could start enjoying our holiday in their country without delay.

We did, four days later, after the hole in the hull of the boat, made by the broken axle when the wheel came off, had been repaired!

As far as I was concerned, a real fringe benefit of taking a boat abroad was that on the return journey it could accommodate all the bulky purchases I had been disposed to make — from plaited strings of garlic bought one summer for a few shillings each, in Spain, as presents for my ever-grateful girl friends, to the huge ceramic plant pots for the garden and a bulky beach umbrella, its cover made of straw which I bore home triumphantly, as the answer to the recession in the East Anglian thatching industry. The chairman of a multiple chain-store who was staying in the hotel when I first acquired the umbrella was so enthusiastic about the scheme that he gave me an open order for the first gross, and I could hardly wait to get home to prove my financial acumen and be hailed as the patron and saviour of one of my country's ancient rural crafts. Unfortunately, my sense of timing was all wrong and the local thatchers, far from under-going a period of depression, were enjoying a boom, thanks to the number of olde worlde cottages requiring new roofs. Still, the beach umbrella looked good in the garden, even though its cover grew increasingly bedraggled with the passing of the years.

* * *

Meanwhile, we were journeying further afield, charting new waters around Mediterranean islands. They were, according to the travel posters, just two hours flying time away, which meant three days away as a boat tows. But we cut down the temper-fraying driving time a little by putting the car, boat and ourselves on the "auto-couchette" for the first part of the journey through France. This way, in theory, we had a good night's sleep rattling through the night in a stifling carriage while the car and the boat were towed along on the open platform attached to the back of the train.

The journey to Majorca was to be "a real part of the holiday this time," my husband assured me: a good meal and a night's sleep on the train to Narbonne, a leisurely two-hundred mile drive to Barcelona where we would spend one night in a hotel and enjoy a day's sight-seeing before embarking on the night ferry to Palma and then driving on, early the next morning, to our final destination.

His enthusiasm was infectious and I prepared for the trip by assembling a most becoming four-piece travel outfit, consisting of a skirt, sun-top, shorts and a long-sleeved shirt in brown, black and white stripes. It was a combination that could adapt itself to any contingency — or so I thought!

I was wearing the complete outfit when we alighted, full of early-morning optimism, from the train at Narbonne to watch the car and the speed-boat on its trailer, driven off their traveling rack, down a short ramp, with indecent speed, by a French rail man. The trailer met the platform with a sickening bump and its boat lurched and slipped perilously, side-ways, to the accompaniment of warning shrieks from the onlookers and some pretty impressive swearing from my husband.

He untied the tarpaulin covering the aluminium boat, a craft which the uninitiated unfeelingly tended to describe as a "sardine tin" and surveyed its carefully-packed equipment. This consisted of a 40 h.p. engine on a special cradle, wedged round with life-jackets, water skis, petrol cans and two batteries, one of which had slipped over on its side. There was no doubt that everything would have to be unpacked to make sure that the contents of the battery had not spilled into the metal hull of the boat . . . It was soon clear that quite a little had . . .

I spent the first two hours in the long-awaited continental sunshine, as the first link in a human chain, man-handling all the equipment out of the boat and, after it had been mopped up, back into it again. For the rest of the day's journey the family argued between themselves just how sinister the effect of acid could be on an aluminium hull, although the liquid had been mopped up within half-an-hour. By the time we reached Barcelona it had been decided, by a majority of three to one, it was safest to unpack the boat again and swab it out with ammonia which, my "O" level son was nearly certain was the correct antidote for acid. I left them to it and borrowed a needle and cotton from the hotel chambermaid to repair a small slit in my new skirt which must have been acquired during the man-handling operations.

Dinner in Barcelona, when we eventually got around to it, was everything everyone could wish for and we were so long sleeping it off the next morning that sight-seeing was irrevocably delayed, partly because, just as we were ready to set out, I noticed two more slits had appeared mysteriously in my skirt, during the night. While I mended them the men decided it might be a better plan to start the day's expedition by driving down to the docks and getting the car and boat lined up for the overnight ferry to avoid the crowds, nearer sailing time.

Eventually, in the full heat of the day we were free from the responsibility of the car and boat and all the luggage, and all set to enjoy the remainder of the day in sight-seeing:

"Lunch first, I think," said my husband, in the taxi, with his usual sense of priorities, and gripped my arm in affectionate enthusiasm. "Good heavens," he exclaimed, "you've got a huge tear in your sleeve."

Suddenly, something was dawning on me:

"What happens," I asked slowly and deliberately, "if acid happens to come into contact with cotton?"

I was not left much longer in doubt: as the day progressed it became a matter of interesting conjecture as to whether I would be left with any skirt at all to wear by the time we boarded the night ferry. We just made it, the skirt and I, but it was a rather sorry affair that I arranged coyly and carefully around me every time I got up or sat down and it was quite a sinister feeling, knowing that bits of my outfit could suddenly and silently dissolve into thin air. During the night, I felt it called for drastic action and borrowed a pair of scissors from the steward.

The following morning, to rather scandalised looks from some prudish Spaniards, I walked down the gang-plank at Palma, wearing a sleeveless shirt and a pair of very brief matching shorts, barely concealed by a rather seductive version of a grass skirt. It just covered the fact that on the right leg of the shorts, the first sinister split had already made its appearance.

★ ★ ★

The only time the boat was left behind on family holidays was when we went to Winter Sports. Here, as with all other athletic activities, my husband's motto was "Start 'em young". Unfortunately, as far as I was concerned, he had arrived on the scene too late to put this into practice as far as my ski-ing went so that, before long, I was relegated to my usual position, bringing up the rear. Nevertheless, for the sake of maintaining family communication, even at the highest level, I tagged along.

So, more often than not on Winter Sports' holidays, did some of the boys' friends whose own parents apparently were not quite so fanatical about the need for communication with their offspring, possibly because the mothers were not the kind who went out to work and spent the rest of the time feeling guilty about neglecting their children. Anyhow, whatever the reason for our large party, it was satisfying to walk into the hotel dining room, followed by about six young boys, and overhear a comment from the next table.

"That poor woman! All those sons! But he must have been married before for you can see the tall one and the dark one aren't hers . . . " Of course the tall one and the dark one were just the two who were!

As the years passed, by trial and error, I managed to develop a satisfactory system of staying with the annual ski-ing holiday, with the minimum amount of effort. My approach was completely different from my husband's. He started preparing himself with knees-bending, leg-raising exercises a good six weeks before the holiday. The bumps and groans as he worked at getting his muscles in trim, echoed through the house, morning and evening, with relentless regularity.

I was invariably far too tired at night

and always in too much of a hurry in the morning, for such indulgence, so I faced the fact that I would have to stagger on to the ski-slopes, worn out with the pre-holiday strain of organising things both at home and at the office, and with my leg muscles conditioned just to the strength of getting in and out of my car, half-a-dozen times a day. But I had made my plans.

The first morning of the holiday, while the rest of the party rushed off and vied with each other as to who could get into the higher class at the Ski School, I quietly slipped away and joined the Beginner's Class.

"Your first time on skis?" the instructor would query, as I laboured breathlessly, trying to put them on.

"As good as," I mumbled, as he bent down to help me and for the rest of the day I would pad around happily in the sunshine on them, feeling my leg muscles stir in disbelief after months of inactivity. Hour by hour, climbing the nursery slopes, my morale rose higher and higher as I revelled in the unfamiliar delight of being singled out as the best in the class. It was a transitory pleasure, for the second day brought the inevitable promotion to Class II.

By then however, muscles toning up nicely, I was ready to use them for the exhausting procedure of climbing on slightly steeper slopes with Class II, for this class was never considered sufficiently accomplished to go the easy way up, on one of the ski lifts. But with the agony, there was still the ecstasy of being one of the stars of the class. It was a heady experience, particularly at such an altitude.

With more than seventeen years ski-ing experience, by the third day of every holiday, I reached Class III where I was doomed to find my true level. This was somewhere towards the back of the class struggling, on a run, to avoid being last in the line and holding everyone up. At this stage it was helpful to try and find a Class III taken by an old instructor on the verge of retirement. In this case, we could soon establish a mutual sympathy in trying to keep the pace slow and the runs short and easy, to the frustration of all the young ambitious members of the class who usually succeeded in getting promoted to Class IV as quickly as possible.

But for me, Class III, with an old instructor, was my spiritual and physical ski-ing home, a state of affairs which exasperated my husband. About the fifth day of every holiday, in his annual attempt to "get me over the hump" and into Class IV where I could at least meet up with the youngest member of the party, he invariably suggested it was time I had a private lesson, and "damn the expense!" It seemed ungracious to spurn his generosity, and motivated by the faint possibility of more "family togetherness", I submitted gratefully, secure in the knowledge that at least the leg muscles were functioning nicely.

But here, I was to learn the hard way that, for private instruction, it was not necessarily safest to choose one of the other ski teachers, in case "mutual sympathy" went too far. Like the day I went on a lone run with an agile 70-year-old lehrer and in all innocence followed him to his little private hut, tucked away, off the beaten track where he kicked off his skis, anxious to demonstrate other things than 'parallel christies'.

"All part of the lesson," he suggested optimistically with the expression of an old sheep dog, anxious to please his master, and when I declined, graciously, he, much to my relief in this lonely snow field, shrugged his shoulders, resignedly and clipped on his skis again. I have never skied faster, or more competently than on the run home . . . except with dear old Ambrose.

Ambrose Biner is one of the great ski-ing characters of Zermatt, the little mountain village huddled at the foot of the Swiss Matterhorn and, like many men in those parts, he seems as ageless as the great mountain itself. I thought he was an old man when we first met and he taught me to ski. Years later he taught my sons and yet today, when they can ski with the best, he can easily outstrip them. Strangely, he looks no different from the first time we met; slim, wiry, and his face the same colour as the everlasting little cigar tucked into the corner of his mouth, for ever creased into a thousand kindly wrinkles.

143

He is perhaps, the most contented man I have ever met. All the winter he skis on his beloved mountains and in the summer he tends the sheep on his brother's fields, just above the little home with beautifully wood-panelled rooms, which he shares with his maiden sister. He was born in the village, into one of its oldest families, and, although he speaks three languages fluently, he would never leave it.

"Are you sad that you never married?" I asked, as we rode in quiet companionship, side by side up to the top of the glacier, on the long ski tow, on our last day's excursion. He considered the question carefully, puffing on his cigar.

"Not any more I'm not. It doesn't matter now," he said.

"How much longer can you be a ski lehrer?"

"I can teach at the school as long as I want to go on," he said, "but I'm not like some of them. When the day comes, at the very beginning of the winter when the teachers go out together to try out all the runs, if I can't ski every run, just as well as the new teachers, I'll give up."

"Will you mind?"

"With that too, it won't matter then," he said, with the profound resignation of a man who lives with mountains. I envied him his acceptance.

My excursion with Ambrose was the highlight of every holiday in Zermatt for, cautious and reluctant skier as I was, only he, and eventually, strangely enough, my younger son, had the capacity to get the best out of me on skis. They would pick an easy way down the most formidable slope and, without forcing the pace, would inspire me to travel at speeds far beyond my acknowledged capability so that, for just a few hours, I was confident and relaxed and caught an echo of the true thrill of a sport that gives old men the exuberance of youth and younger men the illusion of speeding with the gods. A day's ski-ing with Ambrose was a memory to take home, to ensure that the following year I'd be back in the mountains tackling my love/hate relationship with a sport which, I for one, often wish had never been invented.

The last time Ambrose met me was at

the foot of the cable car. He shouldered my skis, in a chivalrous gesture which already made me feel cherished.

"We will have a wonderful day out — day to remember," he promised.

I believed him: nothing would ever happen to me while I was ski-ing with Ambrose.

The cable car carried us up to more than ten thousand feet from where we had the choice of a number of ski tows going up in different directions. From the top of the one we chose we could ski down into Italy.

But the wind came up as we neared the summit and although we climbed the last three hundred feet on skis and looked down across the Theodul Pass to Cervinia, Ambrose shook his head. It was difficult to hear him speak in the strong wind that suddenly whipped up the snow but he indicated it was no day for that trip, motioned me to button the collar of my anourak up over my mouth, for extra protection, wiped his snow goggles and we set off back toward Zermatt.

We were two lone skiers in the swirling white mist, Ambrose ahead and

I following in his tracks, twisting and swinging in faithful imitation of his every movement. This was fun, I thought, as I turned neatly on an icy mogul, swinging round the little hump with almost gay abandon. It was with rather too much abandon, and over I went.

Twenty yards in front, Ambrose heard me go down and waited, a shadowy outline, at the side of the piste. Through the mists of drifting snow, two skiers shot past, the first one completely out of control. He too caught the ice as he turned on a mogul, just ahead and crashed down, ending in a flurry of flying skis, legs and ski sticks, at Ambrose's feet.

"My God," said Ambrose, in a flat, calm voice, "he's taken my eye. His ski-stick has gone into my eye."

He was still standing upright on his skis, but cradling his head in his hands. To my surprise, in his moment of stress, he still spoke in English and, because of this, and the matter-of-fact way he made the statement, at first I thought he was exaggerating, in order to frighten the fool-hardy skiers and teach them a lesson. Then I saw the spots of deep crimson dropping on to the snow, at his feet.

"I can't see a thing," he said. "Not a thing. You must get his name and the place where he is staying. He may have taken my livelihood."

The frightened culprit was a young German. He and his friend promised to report the accident at the ski school.

"Let them go down then," said Ambrose. They did not need telling twice and thankfully disappeared into the mist.

"I still can't see a thing," repeated Ambrose, in a dazed voice, "not a single thing."

I examined the injury: there was a long, deep gash, just under his eye and most of the blood was coming from this. I preferred to ignore a suspicion of blood that was also welling up from inside the lower eye-lid.

"Actually, it's just missed your eye," I announced, with exaggerated conviction. "Missed it by a hair's breadth. It's a miracle. You've nothing to worry about." On top of a mountain, with no-one else in sight, it seemed the only thing to say.

"You're sure," said Ambrose holding his sightless eye towards me, our roles reversed as the teacher, with child-like simplicity, sought reassurance from the pupil.

"Pretty sure."

"Then that's alright then. Already I can see a little with the other eye again; enough for us to ski down."

Down we went, into the mocking sunshine again where there were other skiers. Now and again Ambrose stopped and, removing his goggles, mopped the injured eye with his blood-stained handkerchief. From the bottom of the glacier there was the long ride back to the village in three cable cars, followed by a visit to a doctor who was not quite as convinced as I had been that there was "nothing to worry about".

However, the next day, the eye specialist in the nearest big town confirmed that his eye would be saved. It had been a "Day to Remember" all right, one which neither I nor the man from the mountains will ever forget.

4

Animal Distractions

WHY is it that just when life seems to be organised with things running nice and smoothly, something seems to turn up to restore it to its normal state of sweet disorder — like, for instance, the arrival in our home of Montgomery — or, to give him his official pedigree name, "Bangaline Lionel's Legatee", the troublesome beagle, who just grew more and more handsome?

We certainly never intended to take on the time-consuming responsibility of owning a show dog. It was just that, after a couple of dogless years, we felt the time had come to look for a successor to the long line of cockers and corgis we had either tolerated or cherished, as family pets. This time, for a change, we'd try something a little out of the ordinary, we thought, after much discussion a beagle seemed the answer: it was a manly type of dog and just the right size for our way of life — or rather for our way of life as it used to be, before Montgomery arrived on the scene.

I cannot claim either the credit or the responsibility for picking a prize-winner because, on that far-off carefree day when I went to the kennels to choose him, I was blissfully ignorant about such possible disfigurements as "apple-heads" or "slab sides" and had never even heard of niceties like "well let down hocks" or "a proudly carried stern", just two of the good points which endear Montgomery to judges up and down the country. In fact, it was not until he was a year old and had earned a big write-up in a dog magazine that I took the trouble to find out that his "stern" was really his tail.

In any case, no expert could have known, when Montgomery was seven weeks old, his brow furrowed into a thousand creases and his coat patterned in just black and white with scarcely a trace of the glowing red that would turn him into a spectacular "tri-colour", that he was the stuff of a champion.

I chose Montgomery, in preference to any other puppy in the kennel, the moment I learned that his father was that rarest of all beagles, a stay-at-home with a streak of caution that made him disinclined to wander. I hoped this last remaining son, left in the litter, had inherited this trait. He looked pitifully defenceless and my heart opened to him. I could not have cared less whether, along with his father's temperament, he had also inherited the splendid head of his internationally-famous paternal grandfather, which six months later, it turned out, was just what he had done. But by that time, I and the family had proved quite defenceless, against Montgomery's droll antics, his affectionate good humour, his stubborn wilfulness and, above all, his GOOD LOOKS.

Montgomery just GREW handsome, and not only in our doting eyes: when he was about six months old we took him back to board at the kennels while we went away on holiday. They stared, in stunned disbelief, as he bounded out of the car, jaunty and friendly, the proud culmination of all their years of careful, patient breeding. He licked them cheerfully while they prodded him and nodded their heads and murmured about "showing him" and "giving him his chance" and "reaching his potential".

At eight months old, his breeder checked him over again and, with visions of establishing the name of her kennels on the dog map, stated, rather more forcibly, that it was a shame not to show him. Eventually, in desperation, she offered to do all the showing if I would just try and keep Montgomery in trim and discipline him a little. It sounded a reasonable proposition, so I said I would think about it.

I did more than just think about it: one Saturday morning, just out of curiosity, I sneaked off and secretly entered Montgomery in the local dog show and, later in the day, found myself parading round the ring with some two dozen other "any variety" puppies. I say "myself" because, just at the crucial moment in the proceedings, Montgomery jerked on his unsuitable lead, pulled open its catch and shot out of the ring, accompanied by excited shouts from the spectators of "There goes the beagle!"

He went; out of the hall, down the stairs and into the car-park with me after him. It was the car-park attendant who eventually caught him and had him waiting with his tail wagging aimiably, when I arrived. I dragged him back again, up the stairs and into the ring and, furiously, tugged him through his paces. I apologised, most profusely, to the judge for any shortcomings and explained we were both quite inexperienced and that this was the first time I had ever shown a dog.

"That's perfectly obvious," said the judge, "but don't worry: this dog shows himself." Taking us by the lead, he placed him at the top of the class.

So that was how Montgomery got his paws on the first rung of the show ladder. And how he loved show business! In the ring, he strutted a little more proudly, his tail — or rather his 'stern' — carried a little more jauntily, than the next chap's. But by that time, I wasn't doing the showing: I had handed over that responsibility to his breeder.

I just exercised him every day and took him to dog-training classes, once a week, so that he learned to mix with other dogs. And I also dieted him and loved him, in the completely committed way that only beagle owners can understand.

Even at dog-training classes he was conspicuous because, as a potential show dog, he must not be encouraged to sit down in the ring and therefore, parading round the hall with the other dogs, he alone was allowed to ignore the command to "sit". Perversely, this was the one order he ever really learned to obey.

Although he was a complete beginner, it was by no means my first experience of dog-training classes: as I entered the large drill hall to be welcomed by the yaps and barks of about a hundred pupils, I recalled the time, some ten years previously, when I had made my debut in that same hall, but on the lead of one of Montgomery's predecessors. That was Taffy, a three-year-old Welsh corgi, the family pet who, through no fault of his own, had definitely got a little out of hand. The reason was that no-one, in our busy, disorganised household, had found the time to train him in anything except the most elementary refinements and he had expressed his boredom by embarking on a rapid succession of dog fights and had got involved in chasing cars, worrying sheep and two episodes with chickens. Finally he disappeared on several all-night excursions from which he returned with a nonchalant, dog-about-town air and spent the following day sleeping off his exhaustion.

The climax came however when growls and surreptitious nips met my belated attempts to discipline him by trying to persuade him to move to the back seat of the car to allow my mother to sit in the front one. Like many teenagers, it seemed, Taffy was going through a difficult stage and, unfortunately, at that time, no-one seemed to have produced a book on dog psychology. So I consulted the chairman of the local Dog Training Society who happened to be a keen corgi breeder.

He was quite unperturbed by my stories of the formidable exploits of one of the stubbornest sons of the breed. He showed much more concern at the sight of Taffy's one dropping ear. This had flopped in the heat of his first summer and had never revived to stand up alert and stiff, like his other one, in spite of our attempts to correct it by splinting both ears in sticking plaster for three weeks so that they stood out from his head like a pair of little white horns and friends asked if we had bred the smallest bull on record.

Personally, I liked the drooping ear; it gave him a most appealing expression. But the chairman of the Dog Training Society obviously thought it was a sorry blot on the breed's escutcheon, far more serious than his uncertain temper which it seemed was quite an easy matter to correct. The doggy gentleman hardly bothered to disguise his conviction that I was to blame for both shortcomings and, as a firm believer that there are no problem children without problem parents, who was I to argue? I signed us on for the training sessions.

At the first session, Taffy's collar was exchanged for a metal choke chain and we joined a class of eight dogs and owners and paraded round the hall in a circle, "halting" or "heeling" or "sitting" at a word of command. I had been very dubious as to how he would respond to having potential sparring partners at such close quarters, both fore and aft, as we circled the hall. At his first tentative overture, I gave an inexperienced and over-vigorous tug on his choke, so that he somersaulted clean through the air and landing on his back, with considerable loss of dignity, for both of us.

The instructor came over to sort things out. His sympathy was obviously all on the dog's side. Eventually, we both settled down into something like a working partnership and it was quite amazing how quickly Taffy learned to respond, like the others, to a firm jerk on his chain and gentle pressure from my hand and obeyed the commands with the best. By the end of our first lesson, he could cross the hall at my heels, weaving behind me between other dogs and owners, in a sort of Scottish country-dance, and could "stay" and "lie" with a military precision I would never have believed possible. Moreover, he seemed as impressed as I was with everything that was happening, including the sawdust and shovel that appeared instantaneously to cover up any natural mistakes, and a spectacular display of canine obedience, given during the interval, by the star pupil, a three-year-old sheepdog.

At the end of our first training session, I was told that, given proper encouragement, Taffy could well achieve similar spectacular standards. He never did, of course, but after his first series of lessons, he gave up chasing cars and eagerly came to heel, whenever I called, his eyes alight with the memory of six evenings in his life when, for two hours, he had had my undivided attention.

All that happened long before the days of Montgomery: in between whiles, there had been Sherry, a beautiful, pale gold cocker spaniel, and Jet, his counterpart, in gleaming black. Jet was the unfortunate result of a garden fete I once opened. After the opening ceremony, going the usual round of the stalls, I came across him, sitting bored and dejected, outside a large, green kennel, which bore a label reading "Name Me and Claim Me".

One of the unmentioned responsibilities of opening a bazaar or a garden fete is to patronise, without fail, every single stall and side-show; as well I remember, from one year at the local village fete where a minor highlight of the afternoon was to see if, as opener, I would for once decide to break with this tradition and avoid paying a visit to the cake stall.

The cake stall is invariably the most popular and successful of all such attractions, and to avoid visiting it would certainly have been one in the eye for its organisers, headed by none other than my own daily help, or rather by my former daily help, for just three days before the village fete, she had stormed out of my house, for ever, after having taken exception to one of my more tactless comments about her rather happy-go-lucky method of housework. Of course, the whole village knew all about the incident and were agog to see whether private feelings would get the better of public obligations.

I certainly had no intention of making the slightest move to placate, or even acknowledge, the worthy cake-maker: it was she who was responsible for my having spent the whole of that very Saturday morning doing the week's ironing. All that afternoon she stood, sternly beside her stall, waiting for me to make public obeisance.

Round the other stalls I went, accompanied by the Vicar, to congratulate the organisers and buy some of their wares or try my hand at the side-shows.

"Well, that's it," I said, after the last futile throw at hoop-la, which was the very end stall in the garden. "That's the lot!"

"Yes," the Vicar agreed. "Time for a well-earned cup of tea."

We walked towards the house, the full length of the garden, past the cake stall, the focus of all eyes. Suddenly, the Vicar's courage failed. He too knew the story.

"Dear me," he said, "we've forgotten the cake stall. They will be disappointed."

I stood fast, but he stared me firmly in the eye and, although his lips never moved, I could have sworn I heard him counselling me " . . . forgive them, that trespass against us."

I hesitated. But the fete was in aid of his church. He took my arm and forced-marched me over to the tables laden with buns and sponge-cakes.

"I think you know Mrs H — ," he said, "One of our best workers . . ."

"I don't doubt it," I said, forgetting to shake hands. "It's lucky she has so much time to do all this."

She dropped her eyes, but there were spectators within earshot and I put the knife in, with my sweetest smile.

"You will forgive me though, if I don't buy even one cake. I'm on a strict diet."

Over tea and sandwiches, the Vicar said he reckoned honours were about even!

At the time of the garden fete where I met Jet, Winston Churchill was everybody's hero. I paid sixpence to the dog-minding stall-holder, studied her belligerent looking charge and, with a flash of inspired patriotism, guessed that his name was "Winston".

When the time came to draw the raffles and present the prizes it was announced that it was, although I had strong suspicions that this might have been a piece of pretty swift thinking, on the stall-holder's part, to find a good home for the animal.

Anyhow, surrounded by a garden-full of dog lovers, all congratulating me on my good fortune, there seemed no easy let out particularly as, at that time, we happened to be dogless. So, having been assured that the dog did not bite and had only been parted from his owners through inexplicable reasons, beyond anyone's understanding, I submitted gracefully and left the fete with the enormous wooden kennel strapped on to the roof of the car, the black dog sitting companionably beside me and, in the boot one pound of dog meat to "start him off". It was certainly a more impressive haul of booty than the cellophane-wrapped bouquet and assortment of unwanted groceries and coat-hangers I usually took home from these occasions.

It was soon apparent that my suspicions about his name were well founded; whatever it was it was not "Winston" and after trying him out with a selection of suitable alternatives, we decided he seemed most inclined to respond to being called by a single syllable, so we settled for "Jet".

He, on his part, settled down happily enough and, for the first fortnight or so, we could not understand how his first owners could have allowed him to have been abandoned. We grew quite proud of him and, despite his rather fierce appearance, discovered he was a disarming mixture of affection and independence. One night, dining with friends, some ten miles away, out in the country, we took him with us, in the back of the car. The next day he went missing. That evening, our friends telephoned us to ask if we would please go and collect him from their house where he had arrived, sometime in the afternoon. After this procedure had been repeated, three days running, we quite understood why his previous owners had felt obliged to pass him on. Or thought we understood although, I still maintained, there are no problem children without problem parents. Anyhow, we eventually found him a home with a rough type of country odd-job man who said he would have him with him all day and would stand no nonsense. The last I heard, was that they had come to a pretty good understanding.

Sherry, on the other hand, had been our responsibility since he was eight weeks old. But with the arrival of the new baby, he felt his nose had been rather put out of joint and started going to any lengths to attract attention to himself, even to the extent of taking occasional casual nips at the postman or strange callers who came to the house.

They were only small, token nips and the first person to take real, and no doubt justified exception, was a rather tough character who was going round, delivering circulars. The first we knew about it, however, was when we were served with a summons to appear at the Cromer Police Court, charged with keeping a dangerous dog.

"Dangerous", seemed an outrageous description, so I went to court to defend us. Sherry came too, but I left him in the back of the car, recovering from a violent bilious attack he had had, the previous night. With my years of experience of Police Courts, as seen from the Press Bench, I decided to plead "Not Guilty". When I heard the injured party start to give evidence, I almost changed my mind.

With the light of battle in his eye, he told the magistrates how a great yellow monster had leapt out at him, bared its teeth and sunk them into his left gum-boot. He thereupon produced the said gum-boot, ripped across the top with a series of gashes that looked suspiciously as if they had been somewhat amplified by his own pen-knife. I bided my time. If there was a God who watched over dogs as well as humans, He'd be listening!

When it was my turn to be cross-questioned, I asked the Magistrates if they would like to see the dog. They seemed somewhat taken aback but after a whispered consultation, they rather dubiously, agreed. I went to fetch him and as we had come without his lead, I slipped a handkerchief through his collar, and led him, rather reluctantly, back to the court room.

As the door was opened for us, I had

a distinct impression of the gentlemen on the bench, lifting their feet clear of the floor and fixing their eyes about half way up the door, for a first encounter with "the great yellow monster". Instead, almost crawling along the floor behind me, on the end of a white handkerchief, was a drooping specimen, so weak from his night's indisposition, that he hardly had the strength to stand on his own four feet. There was a moment of stunned disbelief while authority re-adjusted its pre-conceived ideas and the bravest among them proferred the back of his hand to Sherry, as a sort of symbolic olive branch. I lead him over, on the end of the handkerchief and he was still licking the hand, forgivingly, as the case was dismissed. Later, he too, was found a rather quieter home, away in the country.

Montgomery, however had no inhibitions or frustrations: his biggest problem was his weight and, for the first time, I learned the real meaning of "puppy fat":

"A promising specimen, marred by excess weight . . . " read his first official report in *Our Dogs* and at his big time debut, at the East of England Hound Show, he was conspicuous, not only for his splendid head, but because he was, literally, outstanding as the fattest beagle in the ring.

In one last effort to give him a waist-line, and with rapidly falling arches, I stepped up his exercises to two hours of walking a day and, with a touch of inspiration, put him on the diet of hard-boiled eggs that, in a crisis, was guaranteed to absorb my own calories. We were finally rewarded when, in the Midland Championship Show in the autumn, when he was eighteen months old, he made it; that coveted First in Class Certificate that was his passport to Crufts.

From then on, there was no stopping him. At Crufts, that year, I watched with a thudding heart from the balcony, well out of his view for fear of distracting him, as, with perfect poise, he led his breeder to the top of his class, twice over! Afterwards, she celebrated by going off to buy a new hat and I spent the day perched in the edge of his tiny stall on the show bench, basking in the reflected glory of the two red prize tickets, pinned over our heads.

"Henceforth," they said, "the sky's the limit!" But they had reckoned without Montgomery's ideas on the subject: at his next major show, he did the unforgiveable, so I was told, by timing it nicely and rolling flat on his back, right in front of the judge. I wasn't there to see it as, true to her promise, his breeder had taken over the whole of his show career.

Unfortunately, their relationship was severely marred by what happened at the Ladies' Kennel Club Show at Olympia, where he protested at the whole procedure by taking a friendly bite at his breeder, at a crucial moment, just as she was trying to line him up before the judge. I learned later that it took her months to recover, not from the injury but from the disgrace of such a happening, in full view of the country's top-line dog people.

The question was, why should Montgomery suddenly be so determined to make his protests? It was an experienced beagle-owner who put me wise:

"All dogs like a master," he said, "but beagles like an equal," and he suggested that Montgomery was protesting, with all the stubborness of his breed, at being put through his paces by a mere acquaintance when he had a perfectly good owner who should surely share his good times and his bad. If he was in show business, why wasn't she?

Why not indeed? As usual Montgomery got his way.

The eve of next year's Crufts, found him installed with my husband and I, in a luxury West End, London hotel, to ensure that we all had a good night's sleep before the big occasion. The hotel had been surprisingly accommodating when we wrote and asked if we could bring the dog with us. They replied that, providing he was a reasonable size of dog, used the back stairs instead of the visitor's lift and did not go into any of the public rooms, they would be delighted to welcome him. In confirming the booking, we mentioned that he measured just sixteen inches in height whereupon they wrote to say they looked forward to meeting him and they hoped the three of us would have an enjoyable stay.

Montgomery certainly enjoyed his visit. Our night was somewhat disturbed because, in strange surroundings, he insisted on sleeping on the beds and, as usual, was meticulous about distributing his favours equally which, in this case, meant jumping from one bed to the other at hourly intervals.

Seven o'clock in the morning found the three of us walking the deserted streets of the West End, in the pouring rain, while Montgomery sniffed out a suitable spot for his ablutions. When we finally got back to the hotel, he was mud-splattered from nose to stern. Up the back stairs we went — seven flights up — and bathed him in the huge pink bath. He didn't think much of the scented soap which was all we could manage and, although we did our best with it, the pale pink bath sheet looked somewhat out of its element, when we had finished. However, by 8.30 a.m. a rather damp beagle who had managed to snatch half a buttered roll from our breakfast tray, was carried into a taxi.

"Crufts", the doorman announced, in a resounding voice, to the driver and we felt as if we were on our way to Buckingham Palace. That was our first and last moment of elation.

At about noon, I was parading rather apologetically round ring number 6, trying, as number 326 according to the label on my chest, to brazen it out with the best. Of course, we never got so much as a sniff at an award even though I was wearing a bright scarlet trouser suit, in a no-holds-barred effort to catch the judge's eye.

Actually, the judge hardly looked our way, probably because, although Montgomery behaved absolutely perfectly, he was suddenly devoid of all his usual bounce and jauntiness. I suspect that, at the last moment, he was completely overawed at the enormity of what he had done and quite weighed down by having the responsibility of such an inexperienced handler on the other end of his lead.

Afterwards, I sat on the edge of his bench, while the crowds filed past, with hardly a glance. I fed Montgomery chocolate biscuits, to restore his ego and I consoled him with the thought that I would try and do better next time. Oh yes, there was a next time; and many of them. Montgomery, for better or worse, had bitten me with the show bug, and in doing so, had, confound him, committed me to just one more distraction in an already far too over-crowded life.

Gradually, with him, I mastered something of the art of showmanship: there were practical tips, like carrying a piece of smelly sausage roll in my pocket, wrapped in a plastic bag, to prevent Montgomery from getting its scent. If his attention strayed, I had only to rub my fingers in the bag and wave them in front of him, so that he was immediately alert and curious at the enticing smell.

He was a born mimic and I learned to compensate for my failure to give him any form of regular show training, by lining him up, in the ring, behind the first two or three dogs in the class, so that he could watch them put through their paces and be eager to copy. If he was positioned further down the line and had to wait any length of time to show the judge what he could do, he became bored with the whole proceedings and I lost his attention.

To keep his attention and establish a mutual concentration between us was, I learned, the most important part of the show business; making sure he sensed just what I wanted him to do and leaving him, for the short time he was in the ring, to oblige me spontaneously and joyously.

The days out at the open-airs county shows, were truly joyous occasions. Sometimes, it meant driving all through the night, in a luxury private coach, filled with dogs and owners. I was always sorry for the owners of the dogs who were so small that they travelled in special little mobile kennels, or the dogs who were so big that they needed a seat to themselves, or had to sleep on the gangway: Montgomery was just the right size to curl up beside me, on the double seat, warm and companionable, his head on my knee, so that I relaxed and slept for the whole journey and woke up only when we pulled in at a motor-way cafe in the small hours and tumbled out of the coach, half asleep, for coffee and doughnuts, a memory of the midnight feasts of my long-ago school days.

As the sun came up, the coach would draw into the car-park of a strange show-ground and the first priority would be a walk for the dogs, across the dew-soaked grass. Showing dogs is a serious business, at this level; so serious that I found I could never make friends with the owners of other beagles. My friends, with whom I walked the dogs, early on those mornings, were those who owned boxers and dobermanns and were not in competition with me. Montgomery would chase along, between these big dogs and they would indulge him playfully, occasionally bowling him over to check his exuberance, so that he rolled over in joyful somersaults.

For the dogs too, this was a great day out, for which they submitted to being left in their little stalls on the long benches while their owners went to have the traditional show-ground breakfast, set out by eight o'clock, on wooden tables in the big tents; a well-earned feast of coffee and hot egg and meat sandwiches — the best breakfast I have ever tasted!

The judging, for better or worse, was over by lunch-time leaving the rest of the day free for wandering around, stall-shopping, watching displays of country-crafts or fashions, looking at the horses or cattle being put through their paces and meeting up with friends for coffee or drinks in the open air, with all the hours of the day to spare. Thanks to Montgomery I had no shortage of invitations, the year I was entitled to walk round the ground, after the judging, basking in his reflected glory by sporting on my chest a huge emerald-green satin rosette declaiming, in letters of gold, "Best of Opposite Sex".

The question of fatherhood for Montgomery was one that had, on the advice of experts, been deliberately postponed. They felt that as long as he remained in ignorance about the potential delights of the opposite sex the less likely he would be to be distracted from the real business of the show ring by any temptations there might be on hand. Not until he was three years old did we decide that the time had come when he was sufficiently mature not to get his priorities confused and should be introduced to a suitable mate.

There were a crop of excellent candidates but his initiation was eventually entrusted to an experienced old bitch from Cambridgeshire whose championship progeny were already famous throughout the beagle world. Actually, in breeding terms, she was overdue for retirement but the opportunity of allowing her one last litter-to-end-all-litters after a final glorious fling with the splendid young hopeful from Norfolk, was something her breeder just could not resist.

Neither much to my relief, could Montgomery. He was introduced to the rather shapeless Mother of Champions in her owners kitchen where he was so eager to prove his manhood that he never even had time to notice that she had only one eye. It seemed her other eye had been damaged in the litter, soon after she was born and had been removed so that she herself had never made the show ring. I was glad however that Montgomery had not seen her disfigurement.

After the introductions, I was kept too

busy to think about it. Why is it, that where pedigree animals are concerned, the most natural function in the world must be conducted with so much human interference? Forewarned by my dog-minded friends I was prepared early in the proceedings for the bitch's owner to swing Montgomery round, after a judicious interval, so that the couple stood back to back. But nothing could have prepared me for the embarrassment of the next half hour when I knelt beside him, crooning encouraging remarks and stroking him under the chin to persuade him to remain in his position while, at the same time, I struggled to maintain polite conversation with my opposite number, who was holding the bride steady, at the other end of the operations.

Six weeks later as it turned out the bitch had been too old anyway. It was quite certain that she was not in whelp. Could Montgomery return to Cambridge and repeat his performance with a much younger representative of the famous line? He could and he did, in a quietly competent manner that made me quite proud of him. Six weeks afterwards there was a postcard to announce that the young bitch was "nicely in whelp" and could I supply a copy of Montgomery's pedigree, showing his ancestry for four generations?

Bursting with pride, I traced his blue blood back through International Champions to a jolly-sounded "Gay Fellow of Geddisburgh" and his famous great-grand sire "Rossut Triumphant", so called, no doubt, because he rose victoriously over an unfortunate episode on the maternal side involving a possibly aptly-named "Romeo Ripper" and a certain "Fey Fey" a bitch without a trace of red in her ancestory. No wonder Montgomery was a little difficult at times.

The question the postcard raised in all our minds was whether or not, when the time came, we were prepared to face the task of taking on one of Montgomery's puppies? If so, should we have a dog or a bitch? Would Montgomery be jealous of letting another dog into his home? What should we call him? Eventually, after long weeks of discussion we prepared ourselves to receive a dog. He would be called "Blazer"; a neat, sporty sort of name and a fitting reminder of his father's most recent piece of costly destruction.

Alas! If ever there was a case of translating "counting one's chickens" into canine terms, this was it. Even to the experienced eye of the local vet. Chrystabel looked pregnant enough, right up to the last day. But nothing further happened. It was another phantom pregnancy. Needless to say there was no repeat invitation for Montgomery.

At least at first there wasn't, not until he decided to take matters into his own paws: in the Open Class for Beagles in a show organised that summer by the Norfolk and Norwich Canine Society, he met up with yet another representative of the famous Cambridgeshire kennels. It was a small dog show without separate classes for the sexes and she stood next to him in the ring. She was neat, jaunty and provocative, in a way that no bitch has any right to be, in a show ring.

Her handler, my old friend of the kitchen-floor session, firmly denied her charge was even due to come into season; but Montgomery knew otherwise, he was besotted. Fortunately, the judge was a man of the world. He said he fully sympathised with Montgomery for not being able to give him his full attention. It was not the dog's fault and, although each of the loving couple were equally fine specimens, the dog was under the greater strain and therefore he placed him first and the bitch second. Whereupon, the female of the species was lost in admiration at her acknowledged superior and it became a case of love at first sight between them. Even the hardened handler was no proof against the delightful picture they made together.

"All right," she agreed, reluctantly, to my unspoken question. "Bring him over again in ten days time. Perhaps the third time it'll be lucky."

The third time was certainly different, right from the moment we arrived when, studiously averting my eyes from the cause of our previous visit, still swollen with her phantom pregnancy, I led Montgomery out to the wire run in the garden where the true object of affection was barking a riotous welcome; there was to be no kitchen floor stuff this time, it seemed.

I let Montgomery off his lead, he bounded into the run, they greeted each other like long-lost lovers and without delay, he was led off into the darkness of her little wooden hut where we left them to it. It was obvious they didn't need any help from us so we had a leisurely cup of coffee and, half-an-hour later, crept up and peeped through the hut window. They were standing back to back in perfect harmony. I was glad Montgomery had known true love, even 'though, in the end it came to just another phantom pregnancy!

After the disappointment we consoled ourselves that, perhaps, after all, Montgomery had had the best of it, a whirlwind romance that had left him secure against the intrusion of another puppy in his household to threaten his position as self-appointed leader of his human pack. He had also acquired a rarity value by establishing that his qualities, the best and the worst of them, the subtle combination of his breeding and environment, would remain, for ever unique. As usual, he had had the last word!

5

Small Excursions

RUNNING a career, and a home, and looking after a family and showing a beagle, does not leave much time for the refinements of life, like hobbies, or collecting things. But, if I had the time and money to collect paintings and could choose to have the walls of my sitting-room covered with the works of just one living artist, I would, unhesitatingly, settle for Norfolk-born Edward Seago. The irony of it is that, as far as money is concerned, in the early days, when I was a young newspaper reporter and he was recognised as a famous artist, I could have afforded to do just that.

It must so often happen, of course, the missed opportunity and the futile recriminations but, for once, I was so near to it, on that winter's afternoon when we sat by the log fire in his studio and he waved his hand towards the pile of canvases stacked up against the wall and said I could take my pick, at a price roughly the equivalent of my modest week's salary. I should have pledged my earnings for the next three months. Instead, I chose just one lovely little oil painting, showing a view of the Seine, near Paris with the bridge, the Pont Neuf, in the foreground and the twin spires of Notre Dame, away in the far distance. Seago had painted it from the deck of his beautiful blue-green ketch *Capricorn*, with its symbol of the goat emblazoned in gold-leaf on her prow. In this floating studio, he sailed round Europe, but on that winter's day she was moored, like some theatrical stage effect, near the narrow dyke, at the bottom of his boggy garden, in a tiny stretch of Broadland water, leading into the river and from there into the North Sea.

The little painting I bought then was far more representative of the artist's work than the near-life-size portrait of me he had been working on all that winter's day. But it had nothing like the rarity value, for Edward Seago rarely painted portraits and, even more rarely, portraits of women.

"Every woman has a preconceived notion of her own appearance and a preconceived image of how she should look in her portrait," he once told me and added, from bitter experience, "usually, there's the world of difference between the sitter's image of herself and what I see, as a painter.

"If I must do portraits, I prefer to paint men. They have better bone structure and a man's head gives much more scope, in terms of colouring and skin-tone . . . " He waxed enthusiastic: " . . . the blue chin . . . and, around forty, a man's face is like a great map . . . "

On this last score I willingly conceded defeat, but I found an irresistible temptation to be at the receiving end when it came to his insistence on painting a woman's portrait just as he saw the sitter, rather than as she saw herself or as her husband knew her. Perhaps, because as a journalist, I had already been commissioned to do a portrait of him in words, for a magazine, he was willing to reciprocate on canvas, although he qualified his offer by saying he would have preferred to wait and paint me in my old age, which was the only time he enjoyed painting women's portraits, when the face was full of character, irrespective of anything else. But I had no intention of waiting until then, to take him up on his offer.

I had driven to his home, for my sitting. Through the windswept Norfolk countryside and across the marshland, past landscapes that Gainsborough and Constable, Cotman and Crome, had been inspired to paint over and over again and which the man I was on my way to sit for never tired of capturing on his canvas. He, like his predecessors, had settled for this part of England which, because of its wide skies and great cloud formations, its luminosity of colouring and tremendous feeling of space, was the teething ground of landscape painting. With all this wealth of ever-changing material at hand why should an artist, who was financially independent, bother to paint portraits?

But, once upon a time, before he was famous, Edward Seago had chosen to paint gypsies and circus people, and,

I remembered seeing an assortment of rather informal, relaxed Royal portraits. I could hardly wait to see how he intended to portray me.

"In something red," he had said. So I had taken along every single garment I possessed, from a crimson velvet ball gown to a scarlet cat suit. He had chosen a faded tangerine wool shirt which had seen me through a couple of pregnancies. It should have plenty of character!

As the Dutch gables of his Elizabethan home were silhouetted against the sky, over the flat farmland, the prospect of a series of sittings offered a pleasant enough winter diversion. At that stage, I never thought the record-breaking technique with which he captured the ever-changing moods of the skies, could be applied to portraits.

His was my sort of house: I pushed open the high, iron gate and walked up the narrow garden path, noting the brighter new tiles let into the old, red brick walls, evidence of the restoration work the artist had done when he took on the house after the war. At that time, he had also built a huge studio on to the back of the house and lined it with seasoned timber from an old ship. At one end an open balcony divided the high room into two storeys: the balcony storey was used to stack frames and canvases and the space beneath was panelled in oak, like a ship's cabin and provided the ideal "conversation area".

The smell of wood-smoke from the log fire greeted me and the occupants of the two-tier dog basket barked a riotous welcome to the confusion of paint and canvas, books and bronzes, holiday souvenirs and a shelf full of model paper aeroplanes. Edward Seago was busy mixing up paints.

I was told to take up my position in a small armchair on a raised dais, in the middle of the studio. The artist, pipe in mouth, scrutinised me for a full two minutes. He suggested a slight shift of position and then started roughing out an outline in pale paint on the three foot high canvas.

He made an attempt at polite conversation and then, losing interest broke off to fetch a box of chocolates, opened it and deposited it on my knee, as a sort of substitute dummy. Dance music was coming from a radio, somewhere in the background, so I took the hint and lapsed into silence, contemplating a nearly-completed life-sized portrait of a famous general of our time. He looked strangely paternal in unfamiliar civilian clothes and I wondered if he too had eaten chocolates and listened to dance music, or was his conversation more stimulating to creative effort than mine?

The fire and the music and the steady tick from the giant Parliament clock on the wall, lulled me into a sort of stupor until, perhaps a couple of hours later, I was invited to come and look at the painting. I only hoped that my half-asleep feeling had not been commemorated for all time!

On the contrary, at first glance it was a shock to see myself, as in a mirror, but looking far more wide awake than I actually felt. Instinctively, I raised my hand to smooth back a piece of my hair. Neither had I ever considered myself an outdoor type: but, although the painting was only head and shoulders, it gave the impression that I was on horse-back, not sitting in a comfortable chair.

Seago puffed at his pipe and waited for me to comment. My first reaction was one of relief, that I had been let off so lightly; there was nothing wrong with being an outdoor type!

"It's like," he said eventually, and I detected the satisfaction in his voice.

I agreed: it was "like".

"It's just as well," he said. "For if I hadn't got it the first time, it might never have come at all."

The portrait was finished that same afternoon, apart from the background of cloud and sky, which would be filled in later. During the afternoon session, I didn't take up my position on the dais again, but wandered round the studio and was even allowed to paint in one of the stripes on the famous General's regimental tie.

"You really needn't have bothered to have come for a sitting, at all," he admitted. "I could have painted you just as well from memory."

It had been no bother! Ruefully, I thought about the painters I knew who made dozens of elaborate, preliminary sketches of the sitters. It was just my luck to have found the one 'instamatic' one. So much for my dreams of having regular cosy sittings, throughout the winter! Four hours flat and I was there for ever.

"Do you like her?" he asked, suddenly diffident before his canvas.

"I don't know," I said, honestly, studying my likeness. "I don't dislike her though, and one day, I feel I may be jealous of her."

"You needn't worry," he said, "I'll keep re-touching her and paint in the crow's feet, now and again, to keep her up-to-date."

But he never did. Neither, over the years, have I grown jealous of my other self. Perhaps because I never really was the outdoor type.

Yet, the other day, I happened to overhear two acquaintances, criticising the portrait:

"Do you like it?" one of them asked.

"Not really," was the reply. "He's made her look awfully snooty. You can tell he saw some gypsy blood in her somewhere."

When they'd gone, I took a long, hard

look at the red-shirted girl on the wall and found myself grinning at her, not apologetically, nor in self-defence, but rather conspiratorially.

Gradually, over the years, we acquired other Seago paintings; seascapes and familiar scenes with wide, East Anglian skies; and studies of light and shadow in far-away places that I shall never know. Always, the enjoyment of them is heightened for me by being able to picture the artist, standing back from his canvas, pipe in mouth, brush poised after the final stroke, bushy eye-brows quirked, as on that winter's afternoon, to ask and answer the inevitable question,

"Is it like?"

★ ★ ★

Cooking, alas, has never been one of my pre-occupations. But over the years I have, through necessity, been compelled to develop a certain technique that, in moments of crisis, will keep my family content and adequately nourished. The secret lies in giving a "home-made" touch to food that is, in fact, anything but home-made. "Culinary Cheating", is perhaps the most apt description of this short-cut cookery, but it is surprising just how well it goes down, even among friends who pride themselves on their "cordon bleu" qualifications.

In everyday terms, where the family is concerned, the top favourite is "Home-look Shepherd's Pie": the main ingredient for this is one large ready-made shepherd's pie, which can be bought at any good supermarket, on the way to the office. The one proviso is that is should be as near as possible in shape and size to the cook's own pie-dish. Then, it simply becomes a matter of lining this personal pie-dish with a tin of baked beans in tomato sauce, carefully easing the newly-bought pie out of its wrapper, onto the beans and filling in any give-away gaps round the edges, where pie and dish don't quite meet, with instant mashed potato; dotting with butter and heating up in the oven, like the real thing.

Of course, this is the real thing, except a rather pricey version but the expense can certainly be justified by a working wife for whom time is money and blow the expense of using the tin-opener!

Once having embarked on this type of cookery, the first rule of success is to observe the eleventh commandment and "not be found out", even if it means adding a subtle touch of artistry like burning one corner of the Shepherd's Pie to emphasise the illusion.

For special occasions, a fool-proof way of fooling the consumers is to use plenty of alcohol. Too much, of course, and they won't care what they are eating: but, before that stage, a dish like "Instant Braised Ox Tongue" is successful only in direct proportion to the amount of sherry added to the tin of ox-tail soup in which slices of ready-cooked bought tongue can be re-heated with a few capers and tinned carrots.

The main problem, in extending this sort of extempore cooking to more formal dinner parties however, is that, by putting a little sliced tomato here and a squeeze of lemon-juice there and a liberal dose of sherry everywhere, the effect can be so delectable that one of the guests is bound to ask for the recipe. To confess that, less than two hours ago, it was all in the supermarket, is a defeatist policy. Far better to proffer a mysterious look and an evasive answer like,

"Sorry, I'm afraid it's a family secret. But if you really like it, do come again."

It would be an anti-climax to explain that the delicious home-look paté was just a chunk of liver sausage from the delicatessen counter, spooned out into individual portions and arranged, artistically, on a lettuce leaf; or that the iced gazpacho, the soup that the Spaniards make with at least fourteen different ingredients and lots of loving care, and take hours to prepare, was just tinned tomato soup, mixed with equal parts of bottled tomato cocktail.

Harassed housewives are not the only ones who go in for these sort of recipes; house-proud, confirmed bachelors usually have an excellent supply, like Benjamin Britten's symphony of a sweet, a dark treacle jelly made in five minutes flat by adding four tablespoons of black treacle to half-an-ounce of gelatine, lemon juice and sugar to taste, mixed with a pint of water — diluted with plenty of sherry!

On the other hand, going to the other

extreme in the kitchen, something or someone may trigger off an almost primeval urge to create a truly complicated culinary concoction — usually at a most inconvenient time. Like the mention of "Juniper Berries", in an old cookery book. How those words stirred my imagination with their shades of Spenser, " . . . sweet is the juniper — but sharp his bow." I had a compulsive desire to try the recipe, created long before the tin-opener or the wealth of labour-saving devices cluttering up the kitchen. It was a Christmas recipe for spiced beef and how better to introduce a real old-fashioned seasonal flavour into the home?

"Take your butcher into your con-fidence," was the first instruction in the recipe. My own butcher was frankly incredulous when he heard what I wanted:

"Better let me put you a nice piece of silverside in the brine to pickle," he said, trying to placate me and mentally shuddering at the thought of nine pounds of his best fillet of beef going to waste.

I almost weakened, but a momentary vision of the ghost of the capable little housewife who, more than half a century ago, had painstakingly written the recipe down, in her best copper-plate handwriting, and I held firm: I could just picture her looking at me with a pitying expression, from under her morning mop cap!

The next step was to acquire a meat safe, in lieu of a good old-fashioned cellar, for a refrigerator could hardly be interpreted as "a cool, airy place", as stipulated in the recipe. Eventually, a friend said she had an old one I could borrow as she could find somewhere else to keep the dog's meat, for a few weeks. We drove forty miles to collect it, strapped it to the roof of the car and installed it outside the back door on a pile of stones, to the eventual interest of all the dogs and cats in the neighbourhood. By the time, my husband was quite convinced that I was suffering from the strain of working too hard, but decided it was better to humour me.

As for the juniper berries: maybe, in places like Yorkshire, where they grow wild on the moors, they are quite easy to come by, but in Norfolk, it took me a whole day to track down two precious ounces in a herbal chemist's shop.

Eventually, feeling like a general going into battle, I mustered all my ammunition and began operations: the recipe called for the two ounces of juniper berries to be crushed with two ounces of black peppercorns and one ounce of all-spice: then mixed with six ounces of kitchen salt and one ounce of salt petre. This gritty substance was to be rubbed into the hunk of beef which for the past two days had been sanctifying itself for the operation, by soaking in a film of brown sugar.

But this was only a beginning: I would never have believed that a solid lump of meat could demand such attention. For the twelve days of Christmas, I tended it like a baby at bath-time, rubbing the spicey powder into its every crease and corner, turning it tenderly and laying it gently back in its cradle-like dish, in a different position every time.

Possibly, because it weighed just nine pounds, I began to think of it as an almost human responsibility. There was the night when, lying warm and snug in bed, I remembered that I had forgotten to give it its daily treatment.

"One day's neglect wouldn't make any difference," I argued with myself, " . . . or would it?"

With just six more rubbing days to go, it seemed foolish to take a chance. I slipped out of bed, trying not to disturb my husband and, remembering the nights, not so long ago, when, despite feeling sure that the baby's cries meant he was just playing up, eventually, I had to get out of bed, conceding defeat, to make quite certain. Downstairs I crept, and outside, to the meat safe, feeling almost ashamed at turning out into the cold for a piece of meat.

After that, there was little chance of being allowed to forget it, for the family suddenly began to take a genuine interest in the proceedings; this was something far more unusual than stirring the Christmas pudding.

"Have you rubbed the meat yet?" was their first greeting when they came home from school and, if it was a task still to be done, they would stand and watch the ritual, quite fascinated and savour the piquant smell that gradually emerged as liquid began to ooze from the marinating flesh.

On the twelfth day, I took it from its safe for the very last time, rinsed it tenderly and, feeling rather like a cannibal, submerged it in a deep covered pot, in half a pint of water with a little shredded suet, before leaving it to cool in its own juice and then, the final coup de grâce, it was pressed down with heavy weights, to be eaten cold.

I would like to place on record that it tasted delicious. It probably did. But on Christmas night, as it lay before me, on the supper table, so vulnerable on its white doyley and decorated, rather incongruously, with a sprig of parsley, I remembered, irrationally how, just a few nights ago, I had left my bed to tend it. I had a sudden choking feeling and, carefully averting my eyes, I chose a sausage roll.

★ ★ ★

I simply adore weddings, and perhaps because, as a war-time bride, I missed out on having a white wedding myself,

I am for ever seeking compensation, by revelling in other people's; and the more formalities and sentimental trappings about them there are, the more thrilled I become. I never fail to gulp with emotion when the organ peels out and the bride sweeps up the aisle on her father's arm, trailed by a bevy of bridesmaids. I have yet to see a bride who, at that moment, did not look beautiful.

Afterwards, the more tears and speeches there are with the champagne, the better I like it, for even if the speeches are long and corny, they only help to prolong the glorious occasion.

It has been fortunate, therefore, that, in both a professional and a private capacity, I have been invited to hundreds of weddings, including those of royalty, theatrical celebrities and beauty queens, not to mention a couple of circus artists who were married on their tight-rope, balanced thirty or so feet up in the air, with the poor parson elevated onto a platform beside them, on a sort of giant mobile hoist, such as is used to repair telephone wires.

The thrill of the wedding starts the

moment the copperplate, or printed or handwritten or typed invitation, slips out of the envelope and I can begin to plan what outfit to wear. I would travel miles to be there and, in one case, didn't hesitate to go up to the Arctic, for the weekend, to be at the wedding of Hannah, from Finland, who was marrying an English doctor friend of ours.

Their invitation was in both their mother tongues, English and Finnish and it was embossed in gold script on opposite halves of a folded sheet of near tissue-paper-thin, ivory paper. This delicate implication was far too exciting to resist: it meant spending the whole weekend before Christmas, in Finnish Lapland, right up in the Arctic Circle, near the very home of Father Christmas himself.

And so, forty-eight hours before the wedding, we flew into Helsinki with the bridgegroom and his small party of supporters and, from there, by overnight train were carried up to Rovenieme, the capital of Finnish Lapland. There could be few more romantic places in the world for a wedding.

We arrived in that snow-covered world, in time for breakfast and disembarked from the train by the light of a thousand stars. At that time of year, the only evidence of the sun was a pale, bluish daylight that imparted a dream-like quality to life for about five hours in the middle of the day when the snow-tipped spruce stood out, tall and sharp, white silhouettes against the near-twilight sky when every scene became a living Christmas card.

The day-time temperature was twenty-five degrees below freezing. The day before the wedding, we were up in the forest, wearing fur hats and layers of warm clothes, to glide on long, thin skis through narrow woodland paths where the electric lights, high up in the tall trees, took over when the half-daylight faded. Now and again, a little group of reindeer, with bells round their necks, and tame as cattle, crossed our tracks, nuzzling the roots of the trees, for food.

On the wedding morning, the men all went off for a communal sauna, no doubt to further their growing sense of camaraderie as well as to purify their systems, while we women were relegated to the hairdressers, or left to our own devices: I watched the children playing ice-hockey on the flood-lit square, the equivalent of the English village green. Other children were skating or tobogganing on the frozen river which fringed the shopping centre.

It was a remarkably compact little town; more like a village as a result of being completely razed to the ground during the war and, when it was rebuilt, the entire population was rehoused, in a condensed space, in beautiful, modern blocks of flats, instead of houses. There were just two streets of shops, gay for Christmas, but the fur-hatted customers were not buying holly or mistletoe or tinsel for decorating their homes; instead they chose large, brightly-coloured candles to put on their window-sills, to flicker the season's greetings out, through the long, dark, night and scarlet poinsettias and spring tulips and lily-of-the-valley, for inside their homes, as promises of the night's end.

This was the week then everyone was preparing for the serious business of

Christmas: all the parties and merry-making had taken place during the twelve previous days, in an endless round of "Little Christmasses". Now it was time for the housewives to start and prepare the traditional Christmas dinner of pork or ham, served with swede pie and prunes, followed by rice-porridge which, by rights, ought to contain a lucky almond. After the family had all eaten their fill, the remaining food would be left on the table for the following day so that, after Church, they could just help themselves to it, whenever they felt hungry.

Christmas Day was the family day, to be spent quietly, in one's own home. In fact, until recently, it was absolutely forbidden to go out at all, on Christmas Day, apart from going to Church. Boxing Day, however, was quite the reverse. This was the time to visit friends and wish them "Housega Yowla", a Happy Christmas, a greeting which seemed to have a particular sincerity, in the snow-covered Arctic, away from all the tinsel and crackers.

For the wedding ceremony, the large

and surprisingly modern church, was also decorated with traditional Christmas flowers, poinsettias, hyacinths and tulips. The bride, in a long, white gown, carried a bouquet of lily-of-the-valley. She had no bridesmaids or attendants. As she arrived at the great, arched door of the church, on her father's arm, the opening bars of the wedding march rang out and the bridegroom, at this pre-arranged signal, turned from the altar and walked quickly down the long aisle, to meet her.

They met half-way: the groom bowed to his prospective father-in-law, took his bride from her father's arm and led her down the rest of the aisle, to the altar, for the simple wedding ceremony. There was no signing of the register; this formality was something the priest would take care of, later on.

It was quite dark, and the Christmas lights were on in this tiny capital of Finnish Lapland, as we left the church. The seasonal illuminations were white candle-bulbs on the branches of the tall spruce trees and chains of white lights suspended over the main street; coloured lights would have looked too tawdry beside the natural flashes of flame and green as the Northern Lights streaked the sky, for an hour or two, on most nights at this time of year.

From the church, we drove in thick-tyred cars, over the snow-packed roads, into the forest and a rustic cabin where the wedding breakfast had been arranged. A line of flares blazed a welcome through the trees, as we neared this secret place where, just two weeks before, Mrs Golda Meir had held a private meeting with Mr Kosygin.

Inside the cabin, a great log fire crackled as we stood around to drink the first toasts. The language barrier was of no importance when raised glasses and beaming smiles told their own tale. Candles flickered on the six small tables where the thirty or so guests ate a traditional meal of locally-caught fresh salmon, roast reindeer served with sugar-frosted mountain berries and wine-soaked sponge wedding-cake, filled with fruit and cream.

The bride and groom sat apart from the other guests, at a small table for two, in the centre of the room and across both their chairs was spread their "Marriage Carpet", a large rug, woven in blue and red traditional design, incorporating the date of their wedding. As a splendid wall-covering, it would have pride of place in their own home. And again, according to another local tradition, it would be twenty-five years before, as husband and wife, they would be seated next to each other again at a formal dinner-party.

Throughout the meal, a trio of musicians, in national costume, played mournful Finnish folk songs, from an adjoining room. Afterwards, when more toasts had been drunk, they changed to livelier tunes to which the guests performed energetic country dances, inter-spersed with more restful, old-fashioned waltzes.

Of course, there could be no suggestion of "dancing 'till dawn". This was at least some eight hours away when the party broke up in the small hours of the night and left the log fire and the cabin in the woods, to a tradition-loving Finnish girl, who had knitted her own bridal sheets and her English groom who needed no persuading that there could be no better place or time to marry than in the Arctic Circle at "Kaamos Time", the time of the longest night.

Meanwhile, no self-respecting journalist who found herself in the Artic at Christmas time, could fail to make every effort to call on Father Christmas, to write a report on how he was coping with all the childrens' letters, addressed to him, at that time of year, at his home at Kurvatunturi, the highest point in a huge forest, right on the Russian border, according to a large-scale map of Finland. On my map, it was even underlined in red. But when, on the day after the wedding, I enquired at the tourist office in Roveneimi, about how to get there, I found that although Kurvatunturi was just a tantalizing two hundred miles away, it was right in the middle of the two mile forbidden border zone with Russia, and no-one, except of course Father Christmas, was allowed to set foot there.

After the first feeling of frustration, I consoled myself with the thought that it was perhaps, just as well! At any rate, I returned from my weekend in the Arctic with all my romantic notions about Father Christmas still intact and, with somehow, deep down, a conviction that, if he did really live in this country, he had chosen one of the few places, in an over-commercialised world, where Christmas was as fundamental and meaningful as any other season of the year and where the snow really did lie "deep and crisp and even".

★ ★ ★

I remember another wedding, between two people of different countries. The ceremony took place in a stark, evangelical hall in a Norwich suburb and it was the most truly moving ceremony I have ever witnessed. The bride was a tiny, dark Malaysian girl, Irene Sayer. The circlet of flowers on her straight, black hair picked up the pinks and blues of the printed posies, scattered round the hem of her ankle-length, white dress. It was unconventional, as was the whole thing.

A long-haired guitarist in a scarlet knitted pullover, sang and strummed the Beatles' hit number "Here Comes the Sun", as the bride came up the aisle, between rows of wooden chairs, on the arm of her military-looking English father. Her dainty Chinese mother sat on one of the front chairs. Neither was her real parent, but they represented the miracle that she was there at all and about to marry a fair-haired young Englishman.

The whole story began twenty years before that wedding day, even before the bride's adoptive parents were married. Her adoptive father, the military-looking man escorting her up the aisle, had been a Japanese prisoner of war. On his release, he joined the Far East prison service and eventually was seconded from his work, to become a State Resettlement Officer in Malaya.

There, his main responsibility was organising the wholesale evacuation of isolated villages and transferring the inhabitants into large centres so that the Communists in the jungle were denied a source of supply. It was dangerous work; one day, soon after he had taken up his appointment, he was walking at the front of a file of men, when they ran into an ambush which opened fire. Usually, he walked in fifth place in the file, but for once he had decided to lead his men. It was the man in the fifth place who was killed.

There were other such incidents during the months he personally supervised the removal and resettlement of twenty-one entire villages, each with a population of anything up to fifteen thousand impoverished inhabitants who had to be provided with decent homes, community centres, churches and schools.

One day, visiting one of the poorer families who had just been rescued from starvation on the borders of Siam, the Resettlement Officer found the mother of the household, sobbing her heart out, in her new home. It was a lovely home, she said. She was very grateful for it. She was only sad because, the day after they had moved into it, she had given birth to her seventh child and she just couldn't cope with another mouth to feed.

The cause of the unhappiness was a baby girl, thin as a sparrow, with enormous brown eyes in a dusky face.

The Resettlement Officer looked at her and came to the most unexpected decision of his life: he would complete the Malaysian woman's happiness by taking the child.

The woman was overjoyed and handed the baby over, like a discarded doll. The Resettlement Officer signed a bond, accepting full responsibility and immediately delegated it to the dainty Chinese ball-room dancing champion, in Singapore, to whom, somewhere along the line, he had become engaged and who he planned to marry one day, when the time came to retire from his job and settle down in England.

The arrival of the baby somewhat precipitated things and, two years later, he married his Chinese dancer and legally adopted the little Malaysian girl. Five years after that, the whole family settled down permanently in England. It was then that the Resettlement Officer discovered another twist to the East-West fairy tale; he found out that, because of his treatment in the Japanese Prisoner of War Camp, he could never have any children of his own.

"It's a strange thing," he told me, reflectively, "when the good Lord takes it on himself to square up for a wrong-doing, even before you know it's happened."

He must have remembered it all, as, proud and erect, he walked down the aisle, with the accomplished young Malaysian girl who, but for his timely intervention, might only have learned to beg. I too, would miss her after her marriage, for she was my secretary cum Girl Friday. I admired her for many reasons, not least for planning her sincere and unconventional marriage ceremony which had started with a Beatles' hit tune and which ended with a reading from *The Prophet* by the Eastern poet Kahlil Gibran. In her adopted country it expressed so much of her own generation's philosophy on marriage, a philosophy which I too had felt, but never, until that moment, had voiced:

" . . . let there be space in your
    togetherness,
And let the winds of heaven dance
    between you.

214

Love one another, but make not a
  bond of love:
Let it rather be a moving sea between
  the shores of your souls.
Fill each other's cup — But drink
  not from one cup.
Give one another of your bread: But
  eat not from the same loaf.
Sing and dance together and be
  joyous. But let each one of you
  be alone.
Even as the strings of a lute are
  alone, though they quiver with the
  same music.
Give your hearts, but not into each
  other's keeping.
For only the hand of life can contain
  your hearts.
And stand together, yet not too near
  together.
For the pillars of the temple stand
  apart.
And the oak tree and cypress grow
  not in each other's shadow."

6

What the Eye doesn't See

"IF you really want to get into television, you'll just have to get 'blooded'," said a distinguished friend, already making a comfortable living from the medium. It was quite pointless, it seemed, to write around, applying for auditions or asking about possible vacancies; no-one would be the slightest bit interested in a person who had not already proved their capabilities. The whole thing sounded like a vicious circle and I was determined to break into it.

This distinguished friend's own arrival on radio and, subsequently, on television, where his name soon became a household word, had been, to say the least, unorthodox. If he could manage it, handicapped by all those prominent teeth, so could I and, at long last, I was grateful to my mother for insisting, when I was a child, that I wore dental braces!

The other encouraging factor was that, like me, my friend had also started off as a journalist on a provincial newspaper but he had the edge on me, despite the teeth, by being an ex-county rugby player who had once earned an England trial.

With these accomplishments, his chance to get 'blooded' came when a sports writer was needed to do a short commentary for a local rugby Derby. In those days, not long after the war, rugby was considered such a minority sport that it was thought hardly likely that more than a handful of the great British public would be tuned in to listen to the commentary, anyway.

How wrong can you be? After the match, the broadcasting station's switchboard was jammed with telephone calls from rugger enthusiasts, praising the commentary and asking for more. It was obvious that the new reporter's debut had been both a timely and a spectacular success. He had made quite certain that it would be. Before the match, he had taken the precaution of supplying some of his own, personal supporters with handfuls of loose change and persuading them to use it in their nearest telephone boxes, to record their approval in the right quarters, as soon as possible, after the game was over. It was a naive subterfuge, but it worked and he was signed up for three more commentaries.

However, this was hardly the sort of approach that would bear repeating and, anyhow I had no aspirations to be a sports commentator, or, for that matter, a commentator of any kind: I was just curious to try my hand in a new medium, despite my friend's seeming lack of encouragement.

"Perhaps you could have a try at being funny," was his final piece of advice. It seemed that humour was the one thing which was always at a premium, in his business.

My fourteenth attempt at a humorous script seemed possibly, very faintly amusing. More important, my journalist's instinct told me, just six weeks before Christmas it was irresistibly topical and, in visual terms, had also something to offer. I re-typed it, sent it off to a television magazine programme and, one month later, found myself, my mouth dry with nerves, declaring on a mid-afternoon show, how it was possible to tell one's friends' characters from the Christmas cards they sent.

This novel, if highly far-fetched theory, was lavishly endorsed by appropriate illustrations. A very large and ostentatious card, was almost certain to have come from someone suffering from a marked inferiority complex and, as the final touch of irony, would invariably have got slightly squashed coming through the letter-box, so that it arrived somewhat bent, like its sender's own ego.

At the other extreme, as I explained, an extremely small card, not much larger than a postage stamp, could well represent a thrifty, modest type of person who, nevertheless, prided themselves on doing things a little differently.

With really intimate friends, particularly those who bought their cards in bulk and sent an identical one, ready printed with their own address, to everyone, it was markedly significant, I suggested, how their choice of card ran true to type over the years, to such an extent that it was often possible to identify a close friend's card the moment it came out of the envelope, just by the picture and without reading the name inside.

Any sudden out-of-character variations in these friends' cards could be most significant: for an example, on the screen appeared a picture of a red-nosed chef, bearing aloft a succulent boar's head for the Christmas dinner. I had been taken aback to receive this card from a very artistic friend who usually chose to send something far more delicate and subtle. Eventually, I learned that she was slightly pregnant when she chose her boar's head and so was, probably, more pre-occupied than usual with fundamentals like good solid food. Proof positive of my theory came the following year when her card, like her waist-line, was back to normal!

Similarly, out-of-character cards could well indicate some crisis in the life of the sender; the illustration that came up on the screen was a cartoon of a couple in an old car and, tied on behind them was a tricycle ridden by a stout old lady. This card had been sent by a married couple who invariably chose a picture of a calm, traditional snow-scene to convey the compliments of the season. This year, as it eventually transpired, they were unwittingly announcing to the world that their own lives were being severely complicated by a mother-in-law problem.

But there were subtle pitfalls to avoid in this facile method of character-reading. I showed a picture of a gentleman poodle kissing a lady poodle, under the mistletoe. At first glance, this could have been the obvious choice for a gay dog type to send. But years of Christmas cards analysis had taught me it was much more likely to have come from someone who liked to picture himself as a bit of a gay Lothario. The real wolf or gay dog was far more likely to be lurking behind a picture of a conventional flower arrangement or a respectable reproduction of a painting by an Old Master. Meanwhile, the die-hard, non-committal gentleman, afraid of putting a foot wrong, could be relied on to send discreetly-crested club or regimental cards, or ones from their old school, with carefully-knotted ribbons, which looked just about as festive as my bank statement, particularly when this was liberally dotted with red numerals.

There were many other examples: I showed a scene from the ballet, from a colourful, dramatic personality, who loved to be in the limelight and had a rather theatrical approach to life; and a jolly Father Christmas, loading his sleigh with toys, from a middle-aged couple who seemed determined to cling on to childish things, possibly because life had not quite measured up to their younger expectations.

By this time, I was well into my stride and, nerves forgotten, was almost enjoying myself, until the power-that-be in the producer's gallery had presumably had enough and the floor manager gave me the signal to 'wind up' in one minute's time: I automatically acknowledged his signal with an un-professional wave of the hand and advised the world, or any part of it that happened to be looking in at two o'clock on a mid-week afternoon, to try this theory out for themselves, as good, clean family fun, round the fire on Christmas afternoon.

It might have been even more fun, in Victorian times when the fashionable

Yuletide greetings often looked more like Valentine cards, displaying a love element which was not necessarily of the platonic kind. To illustrate this, I ended with an example which was my piece de resistance; a Victorian Christmas card showing a nude maiden, standing coyly and appealingly, in a pool of water, endorsing, rather unseasonably, the sentiment "My Love I Send Thee With My Christmas Greeting."

It would have been satisfying to have been able to report that my television debut was a sensational success: but, I will never know, even though, following in the footsteps of my distinguished friend, I also had taken the precaution of arranging a comparable follow-up. It took the shape of distributing, in advance, a modest amount of personal fan-mail, to friends in various parts of the country, with instructions to post it back to me, at the studios, after they had seen my performance. And, in line with the spirit of my item, most of the fan-mail took the form of actual Christmas cards.

This, I felt was the master touch, although it turned the whole operation into rather a costly one: I bought cards and stamps and more stamps to send back the self-addressed fan-mail. But, no-matter, I was sublimely confident the whole time-consuming procedure would prove worth-while, in the long run. As things turned out, I did not have to wait long to see the results.

Just ten days after the broadcast a bulky package arrived at my home. It contained fifty or so cards and letters, all addressed to me, in the various specimens of my own disguised hand-writing. Not one of them had been opened. Only in the fullness of time, did it transpire that it was the usual procedure to forward, unopened, all mail addressed personally to individual performers.

I had learned my lesson and, although the manoeuvre failed, I had been right in my assessment that one of the best criterions of a successful broadcast is the amount of audience reaction it creates, in terms of letters and telephone calls. Nevertheless, I am constantly amazed, even humbled, by the numbers of people prepared to go to trouble and expense to air their feelings — if not always in the most flattering or nicest, possible way.

However, any reaction is better than no reaction at all and even the most abusive letter can serve a pretty useful purpose, if only by helping to keep a performer's feet firmly on the ground, with this sort of typical example, from a woman listener, which I received after an early morning radio broadcast:

"I have just listened to your early morning programme and it really is pathetic. You should teach your Grandmother to suck eggs . . . I have listened in the past and felt shocked, I can assure you, at your ignorance. The majority of your listeners must cringe, as I do, when I listen to your banal remarks. I do try and listen without prejudice, but you really make me see red at times . . . You should think twice about what you say on the air. Now I have that off my chest, I feel better."

The ultimate aggravation which had triggered off this writer's fury, had been, I suspect, that I, a mere Yorkshire woman had told her, a Norfolk woman, how to make dumplings! Reading the last sentence of her letter, however, gave an indication of how many people there are who, for one reason or another, have a very real need to express themselves to another human being.

By far the greatest number of these are the old people, who are often lonely and alone. There was one dear old soul, a doctor's widow who, every week when it was my turn to present the early morning programme, could be relied on to telephone at least once, as soon as I came off the air, under the pretext of offering me a recipe to use in a future programme. She had, in her time, been something of a cookery expert and, as such, had done quite a few broadcasts. One day, I went along to her flat and made a recording of her telling some of her old recipes and afterwards, spent quite a time, editing and condensing it into a crisp enough form to broadcast. When it was used and we sent her a small cheque, she was highly indignant:

"I just enjoyed being asked to talk," she said, and ever afterwards, whenever she gave me a recipe over the 'phone, she prefaced it with the warning.

"Now mind you don't send me any money if you decide to use it."

The amount of correspondence from old people reached record proportions after my investigation, on radio and television, about the various types of accommodation for the elderly that were available in this country. These ranged from incredibly stark institutions in converted workhouses, run by the local authorities, to luxury self-contained flatlets, equipped with the most modern labour-saving devices and where help was always on hand at the touch of a bell. Yet, in nearly every case, the old people's homes happiness largely depended on the attitude of the people who were running the home, more so than on the amenities.

For many months after this series, letters from old people poured in and not all were asking for information about the actual homes. Most of the correspondence came from lonely men and women, in all parts of the country, who just wanted to tell someone of their own troubles and anxieties. Although each letter had to be acknowledged, it was obviously quite impossible to become involved in the pen friendships which, I suspected, was the one thing most of the letter-writers would have most enjoyed.

Perhaps, one day, someone will consider running a correspondence club for the elderly, for those who have no-one of their own in the world to write to, or whose children do not manage to communicate with them nearly as often as they would like.

As for the abusive letters: justified or not, some of the sentiments they express do, eventually, encourage personalities in the public eye to develop fairly thick skins, as a means of self-preservation, even if they have no bearing on the reason why some celebrities wear dark glasses in public. They do so not always, as many people suspect, either for disguise or to attract attention. They are, quite simply, a most effective means of avoiding the curious eyes of complete strangers who recognising them from the television screen or the films don't quite know what to do about it, apart from making the inevitable comment:

"I know you, but I'm quite sure you can't possibly know me," to which I have never yet heard the satisfactory answer.

★ ★ ★

Any television personality in danger of suffering from a delusion of grandeur should be subjected to the sort of treatment I received at the hands of one of the most venerable of our East Anglian peers. He was a great character who not only owned one of the finest private art collections in the country, but could trace his ancestry back to some of the Kings of England, albeit on the wrong side of the bedclothes, as evidenced by the magnificent family portrait in the entrance hall, showing some of his antecedents, neatly labelled. "The Natural Children of King Charles II."

I studied it as I waited in the hall, one bleak, winter's afternoon, with my camera team. We had driven through the magnificent parkland, laid out some two hundred years ago by the great English landscape architect, Capability Brown, as a setting for the great stone mansion, large enough to house the entire village, church and all.

There had been no sign of life as we drove through the gardens and pulled up at the front door. We had tugged the iron bell-pull and a dog barked as the bell clanged away, somewhere in the far distance. After a long pause, slow footsteps had shuffled towards us, from the other side the bolts had rattled back, the door had opened a shade and a little bent old man, with white hair and wearing a tail coat, had peered out, blinking short-sightedly.

Yes, we were expected; would we please come in and wait? He bolted the door behind us and, indicating we should wait in the hall, disappeared through a little leather-covered door, while we studied the family portraits.

In a little while he returned and motioned us to follow him through the leather-covered door, into a narrow, stone corridor. He hobbled ahead. I caught a glimpse of great reception rooms, shrouded in dust sheets and a dining room where, according to my home-work, the French traveller de la

A seal pup on a sandbank in The Wash – a silky cuddle of beige and white fur like a character out of Disneyland. *The Universities Federation for Animal Welfare.*

Ambrose – the most contented man I have ever met.

June Hamilton and Roma Lester – Queens of the secondhand clothes business. *Norman Eales.*

Jack Barrett –
Fenland Storyteller. *Peter Doubleday.*

Dorothy Thompson –
fiercely independent. *Theodore Greville.*

Horace Bull –
veteran angler extraordinary.

Ada Roe of Lowestoft at 111,
the oldest woman in Britain. *Ford Jenkins.*

Banquet with fellow journalists at the *Old George and Dragon*.

Farrolds.

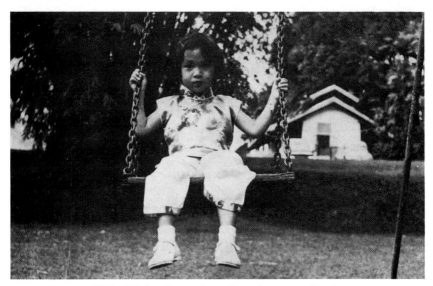

Pik-Yuk shortly after her arrival.

Pik-Yuk.   *Peter Le-Britton.*

Rochefoucald once dined. Afterwards, he wrote in his diary;

"The sideboard is furnished with a number of chamber pots and it is common practice to relieve oneself whilst the rest are drinking; one has no kind of concealment and the practice strikes me as a little indecent."

Me too. But I had memorised the story with the forlorn hope of getting his Lordship to relate it in front of the camera.

We pressed on; through other doors I saw huge stone kitchens and dark pantries and still-rooms and a coal cellar. It took a dying breed of Britisher to chose to exist in such maximum discomfort. It was cold and dark and slightly musty and it conjured up memories of the time when I had been down a coal-mine and there had been a long walk, along a brick-walled corridor, to the coal face. But those walls had been white-washed and it seemed much cleaner.

Eventually, just when I was realising that I could never have found my own way back to the front door, our guide knocked at a door and, to a gruff

"Come in", we found ourselves in a large, pleasant sitting-room. Our host and three ladies were sitting round the fire. The fine-looking eighty-year-old aristocrat rose to greet us. He introduced us to his two sisters and a friend and then, excusing himself to the ladies, led the way to his study to show us the painting which we had come to interview him about, on television.

The old black-suited retainer was still with us; he seemed to be the only servant in this great, cold barn of a place.

"How many will there be for tea, my Lord?" he enquired, before he left us. There was a pause, while the heads were counted: I had a warming vision of tea round the fire with traditional English fruit cake and grinned optimistically, at my producer, the camera man and his assistant.

"There'll be just four," our host said, rather absentmindedly, but I didn't bother to correct him. Anyhow, perhaps he didn't indulge in afternoon tea.

Meanwhile he was delighted to be giving an interview to be used on television: it was something he had always wanted to do. No, he hadn't a television set, so we must tell him exactly what we wanted him to do.

He was a marvellous pupil, or rather the ideal natural performer who liked nothing better than being invited to explain the finer points of his beloved paintings. Within a couple of hours we had most of the required interview "in the can". The butler's return was well-timed;

"Tea is served, my Lord," he announced with dignity.

"Thank you, James," he turned to us, and I picked up my handbag.

"You will excuse me then, while I take a little refreshment with my sisters and our friend?" and, with a courtly bow, this aristocrat, who had never even considered the possibility of sitting down to eat with television people and to whom the medium was just an amusing new-fangled triviality, strode, quite nonchalantly, from the room. Ever afterwards, whenever I see a painting by Stubbs, I think of a piece of traditional English fruit cake I never had!

Similarly whenever I see children making sandcastles on the beach I think back to the most embarrassing moment in the whole of my career as a television journalist. It took place on the beautiful, golden sands of Yarmouth and was at the hands of a gentleman by the name of Mr Bultitude who, by profession, was none other than Great Britain's last remaining sand artist.

For as long as anyone could remember, his splendid relief models, in fine, golden sand, of sea-lions and famous personalities and voluptuous mermaids had been spread out on his regular pitch, just below the main promenade. All the summer, an unending procession of seaside visitors could pause to enjoy his artistry and, if they felt so inclined, show their approval by tossing a few coins into his up-turned cap, by the side of his masterpieces.

But fashions change, even in seaside holiday magic and the newest generation of promenaders did not respond as their predecessors had done, even 'though Mr

Bultitude up-dated his ideas a bit by portraying scenes from television epics, instead of Mickey Mouse. Eventually, came the day when Mr Bultitude let it be known that, owing to lack of public support, he had reluctantly decided that the time had come for him to retire.

His decision, like the end of the music hall in the theatre, represented the end of an era in seaside entertainment; of penny peep shows on the pier with their spicey offerings of "What the Butler Saw" and the last dramatic moments of "The Execution", when the hangman's knife fell. It heralded the beginning of the end too for the few straggling donkey rides and Punch and Judy shows: it promised the ideal off-beat story to include in a television holiday round-up at the height of the summer season.

Mr Bultitude was more than agreeable to the idea: indeed, he welcomed it as a fitting conclusion to his long and unusual career. For days before the broadcast he was hard at work, designing and perfecting his final masterpiece: it occupied the whole of his square pitch and was a splendid scene of a train of galloping horses, manes flying, drawing a Wild West wagon across the sand. Oh, that such talent, like that of pavement artists', could have been channelled into a more permanent medium!

When the day for the programme arrived, our television cameras were set up, on the promenade, just above this masterpiece and I started to rehearse the artist to get him to condense his life-story into the four or five minutes screen-time at our disposal. It had been decided that the camera would open up on a shot of Mr Bultitude, pretending to put the finishing touches to one of the horse's tails. It would pull out to reveal the whole picture, with me admiring it. After a suitable pause, I would interrupt Mr Bultitude's work by proferring the million dollar question;

"Tell me, Mr Bultitude, why, after working here for nearly half a century, have you suddenly decided to retire?"

As usual, when the television cameras are set up in public, a crowd had collected around them. For holidaymakers, in particular, this was the ideal form of free entertainment, on a warm, sunny evening and, by transmission time, the spectators were four deep along the promenade.

With five minutes to go, I went over the opening move with Mr Bultitude, for the very last time. He was word perfect; almost too perfect, but it couldn't be helped. With ten seconds to go, the red light glowed on the camera; the producer cued me and we were on the air. Mr Bultitude was confident enough, chiselling away at a few stray hairs on the horse's tail: I watched him for the appointed ten seconds, before walking into shot to surprise him with,

"Tell me, Mr Bultitude, why have you decided to retire?"

It was I who was in for the surprise: he stopped his chiselling, straightened up and turned, on cue, slowly and deliberately, to face me and the camera and the crowds on the promenade and the waiting world in their homes. Thoughtfully, he rubbed his chin and contemplated them all. He paused and even took off his cap and scratched his head. What an actor! I congratulated him, mentally, until the thought dawned on me that me might just have forgotten his lines.

But no: he fixed me with his eye and there was a gleam in it I had never seen before.

"Dear God!" I thought. "We're going to get our money's worth this time."

"Retire?" said Mr Bultitude, and grinned toothlessly. He surveyed the crowds again, but this time with an expression of smug satisfaction.

"Do you know," he confided, "it's just like the good old days? And seeing has 'ow all these people are so interested in my work again and seeing has 'ow I'm going to be on the telly, all of a sudden like, I think I've changed my mind."

* * *

From the seaside too, came another television personality to catch me with my trousers down, or as good as, in the most literal sense of the expression. He was a little grey seal, just a pup; silky cuddle of beige and white fur, only a few weeks old. His round, brown eyes blinked myopically in the studio lights. Their flat, saucer-like look which gave him such a helpless appeal would have enabled him to see excellently below the surface of the sea, but in this strange environment, he seemed pathetic and vulnerable and there was hardly a secretary in the building who had not come to stroke his absurd, round, shiny little head; he was like a character who had strayed from Disneyland.

He had, in fact, strayed from much closer at hand; from the inhospitable shores of Scroby Sandbank where he had been born on that finger of land that appears only at low tide, a mile and a half out in the North Sea. A few hours after his birth he would have been able to swim and float at the side of his mother but he must have fallen asleep and a strong current or an unusually high tide perhaps, had swept him away from her. Anyhow, he had been washed up on the mainland where, on waking he would have attached himself to the first person he saw.

Fortunately, for this particular seal pup, he had been taken along the beach, by his finder, to a special "nursery" for baby seals where he had been fed a carefully-devised diet of cow's milk, mixed with liver and whale oil. Because he could neither lap milk from a saucer or suck from a bottle, like most mammals, the mixture had to be fed straight into his stomach through a tube inserted down his throat. He was being kept in the nursery for a month or so, until he reached the age when he would normally have been abandoned by his mother when he was old enough to catch fish and fend for himself. At that age, it was planned to take him out to sea in a boat and release him, several miles off the shore.

The scheme was practical enough. The only problem was that seal pups are ridiculously friendly creatures and, in practice, it turned out that they usually persisted in following the boat and their mother-substitute, back to shore again. However, the survival system was worth trying, according to the Inspector from the R.S.P.C.A. who had brought this particular pup along to the television studios, in the back of his shooting brake, to get a little publicity for the seals' nursery and impress on the general public that, if they found a little seal washed up on the beach, the kindest thing was to notify his organisation rather than take the lovable little creature home and try to keep it in the bath and make a pet of it.

It was most understandable why anyone would try and make a pet of the little pup who lay so contentedly across my knee, waiting to make his television debut. He was surely the most attractive of all young creatures. I stroked him, tenderly and he was quiet and relaxed, lulled perhaps by the hot lights of the studio.

I felt a warm glow of admiration for the independent little orphan; a warmth that suddenly, he seemed to reciprocate. I felt it first, somewhere near the top of my legs, a hot, moist sensation that spread over my legs and seeped through my lap onto the chair. At first, I did not quite register what was happening and then I identified the experience with a memory of long-ago days, when my sons wore nappies — or rather, should have been wearing nappies. But in those days the outcome was never quite as traumatic as this.

Already there was an unmistakable trickle of water on to the floor; I felt, or rather heard, it gaining momentum. So did the R.S.P.C.A. Inspector, sitting in the opposite seat, waiting for the interview to start. But he was a stout-hearted chap, used to all animal emergencies and he did not flinch as I posed my rather breathless first question. Once started, he battled on with his story about an old man he knew, who had lived in a cottage on the coast and had tried to rear a tame seal by letting it sleep on his bed.

"Not possible," I longed to shout, past caring about the well-being of any seal and literally glued to my seat by the fishy-smelling liquid that was still pouring from the docile animal on my knee and had formed into a small pond on the floor which was spreading out and looked like turning my chair into an island. How could one young thing produce such an impressive volume and would it ever stop?

It did; at the exact moment the Inspector finished telling his story with its tear-jerking climax of the man coming back from holiday to find the seal lying dead on the verandah. With a sympathetic look he waited, expectantly for my next question. But I had had enough. I had not the faintest idea whether the cameras had been showing the scene below knee level, but I was past caring.

"Don't worry," I choked. "There's not the slightest danger of my ever trying to make a pet of a seal pup — or anyone else with any sense, who's watching this programme." And, just in case there was any misunderstanding, I pointed to the floor, with a flourish:

"You do realise, I hope, that this mess is him — not Me."

★ ★ ★

Even recording interviews for radio, on a portable tape recorder, produced their share of embarrassing moments, usually when the machine seized up at the most inopportune moment during a scoop interview, after days of preliminary negotiations.

There was the time the premier Baronet

of England discovered that a little oil painting which had been hanging on his walls for generations, was a priceless Old Master and I was lucky enough to be first on the scene to persuade him to be interviewed about his "find": I had cornered him in his study, between breakfast and the first appointment of his very busy day and, rather reluctantly, he agreed to do the interview there and then. The tape recorder was even more reluctant: it refused to perform at all.

For endless minutes, I fiddled ineffectually with the controls, checked the batteries and finally, in a last despairing gesture, picked the whole thing up and dropped it from a height of about two feet, a trick which occasionally had been known to startle it into action. But not this time. Having come to the end of my repair repertoire, I conceded defeat, thanked Sir Edmund Bacon gloomily and packed away the cause of my abortive journey.

"No interview?" said Sir Edmund.

"'Fraid not," I muttered, feeling distinctly foolish after all the arguments I had used to persuade him to talk. "They wanted the interview by mid-day and by the time I go back and collect another machine and come back here again, it will be too late."

He rubbed his moustache reflectively, musing, I suspected, on his unexpected reprieve from the unwelcome publicity. But I had misjudged him; I had taken no account of the good old British chivalry coursing, with the blue blood, through his veins.

"Come along," he announced, decisively; "If I can get there and back within the hour, I'll come back with you to your office and you can get another of these confounded machines and we'll do the interview on the spot."

It was an easier way out of the trouble than the time my tape recorder packed up at the Foreign Office when I had gone to interview Lord Caradon, then United Kingdom representative at the United Nations. The interview had been preceded by several transatlantic telephone calls and was to take place just a few hours after he had flown in from America when he could spare me just ten minutes from his, understandably, very over-crowded time-table.

I had been through all the Foreign Office ritual of being signed into the building and conducted through its dark gloomy corridor of power to a small, impersonal boardroom where I set up my tape-recorder, tested it, and was all ready for action when Lord Caradon, blue-eyed and sunburnt, walked in precisely to the minute. We discussed the proposed line of questioning: then I switched the machine on and, unbelievably, nothing happened. Resisting an overwhelming temptation to scream and rush out, I focussed all my attention on going through my sketchy emergency routine. Still nothing happened. I switched off: I knew when I was beaten.

"Sorry sir," I said. "It's not my day."

The expressive, bushy eyebrows shot up in astonishment and the blue eyes blazed. I felt quite weak.

"Not your day?" he barked, explosively. "We don't give up all that easily at the Foreign Office."

He reached for the telephone. There must, he said, be another tape-recorder in the building.

"Get me the Press Department," he requested the telephonist. I sat back and let everything happen. It did.

Three minutes later, a tape recorder was on its way from the Press Department. Lord Caradon went off to his meeting with the Foreign Secretary and I was left with the promise that in exactly fifteen minutes time, he would make some excuse to leave the meeting and come back for precisely five minutes, to record the interview.

There was just one unforseen snag: when the tape recorder arrived, it turned out to be a brand new one, still inside its cellophane wrappings, in its cardboard box. Moreover, it was a model that I had never seen before. Fortunately, the instruction book was with it, so while the young Press Secretary, or whoever he was who had carried it in, read out the instructions, I tried to find my way round the controls. I had just about succeeded in getting the wheels turning, I hoped effectively, when Lord Caradon returned.

"My dear young lady," were the first words on the tape, "you don't think the

Foreign Office can be silenced by an obsolete tape recorder."

★ ★ ★

With 'live' television interviews with human animals, a real potential hazard comes from fortifying the interviewee with one alcoholic drink too many and I can recall just such an occasion when this really jeopardized a programme. It involved an over-conscientious medical officer of health who had come to the studios to be interviewed about a sudden rise in the number of cases of venereal disease, in his part of the country. In the beginning, he was more than keen to publicise this worrying state of affairs because of the need to alert public attention. But, in the studio, it was another matter: the jovial doctor suddenly lost a good deal of his enthusiasm and became as guarded and reticent as a criminal in the dock. He obviously regarded his imminent television debut as a fearsome ordeal.

His symptoms were classic: he mopped his glistening forehead, licked his dry lips and, rather apologetically, asked the inevitable question; "What happens if I dry up". There was very little danger of that: every interviewer has a stock of questions, guaranteed to elicit more than monosyllabic replies of "Yes" and "No".

The unspoken and perpetual query, in cases like this, was what would happen if a middle-aged victim, evidencing acute symptoms of strain and anxiety, had a heart attack, during the interview? Fortunately, there seemed to be no precedent for this catastrophe and it was certainly not the opportune moment to pursue the theory with this particular medical expert, who, fortified by a stiff whisky, was showing signs of recovering his equilibrium and was turning a distinctly better colour.

He had a good story to tell and knew his facts inside out: he could hardly go wrong, providing he could just relax sufficiently to do himself justice. Meanwhile, he had done full justice to his first whisky and he accepted an invitation to have another, with the confidence of a man who certainly knew his own capacity. With ten minutes to go before the broadcast, I left him to it and disappeared to make a 'phone call. When I returned the good doctor was contentedly sipping his second whisky. Or was it his third? The bottle beside him looked rather more empty than I seemed to remember. No matter; if a medical man could not judge his own capacity, who could?

He was certainly confident enough, by the time we were on the air: in reply to the first question he was jovial and expansive, a real "father figure", 'though perhaps just a shade too expansive, but it was better that way. And then, the noise began; a dreadful creaking, clanging sound that punctuated his every sentence as he leant forward, to emphasise a remark, or swayed backwards, relapsing in self-satisfaction at his own answer, to wait for the next question. Each time he moved there was the sound; something between a groan and a metallic crunch which re-occurred with alarming regularity, at the beginning and the end of every single one of his observations.

The floor manager was transfixed with

fascinated horror; a camera man took his head-phones off, examined the ear-piece and, finding nothing amiss, poked his finger in his own ear and wriggled it about, exploratorally. I tried to take a mental grip as I felt myself losing the thread of the interview. But still the eerie sound persisted. The only person who appeared quite oblivious or unconcerned, was the doctor himself: like an armoured Don Quixote, he was battling on, well away, trying to put some of the wrongs of his world to right. He looked completely crestfallen, the wind taken out of his sails, when at a signal from the floor manager, the interview ground, quite literally, to an abrupt ending.

"O.K.?" he asked, cheerily, as soon as we were off the air.

"Yes," I lied, "apart from the rather strange creaking sound. Did you hear it?"

"Oh, Lord!", he said. "You mean this noise?" and he thumped the lower half of his leg with a metallic-sounding slap and, gripping it firmly, he pulled it backwards and forwards, to reproduce the loud, grinding creak.

"My tin leg," he explained. "Needs a bit of oil and I expect I forgot to lock the old knee in position . . . " and he repaired the omission with a sharp click. But that artificial limb was not the main cause of his swaying gait as he wove his way out of the studio, not the reason why he was prevailed upon to go home by taxi and leave his car, to be collected the following day.

* * *

It was not the whisky bottle that endangered the television interview with a neurotic and highly-strung famous authoress whose publishers had arranged a whirlwind personal appearance tour for her, to promote her latest best seller. The book was about her travels with a circus but, on the eve of publication, her favourite lion in the circus, who was one of the main characters in her book, had met with a fatal accident. This, it seemed, had triggered off her near-hysterical state so that just the mention of the animal's name was liable to reduce the authoress to floods of tears, or so I had been warned by her agent.

We met each other, the authoress and I, an hour before the broadcast. The good lady certainly was emotional. She wrung her hands and talked in a rather breathless, inconsequential manner, apologising repeatedly for her bad nerves. She blamed them on the fact that, for the past two weeks, she had been living out of a suitcase.

Whatever the reason, she was a pitiful figure. She reminded me of the young pop singer I had interviewed years before and who I afterwards suspected was being slightly exploited by his unscrupulous manager. This frail young singer was topping the bill at a seaside summer show. He was just a slip of a lad from the North Country, but with a microphone in his hand and the spotlight playing on his fair hair, he offered a brand of vulnerable magic that sent the fans wild.

Perhaps, because he had caught the faint Yorkshire timbre in my voice and sensed a fellow Northerner, he telephoned me at the studios, the day after the television programme: he felt he just had to talk to someone; he didn't know a soul in these parts and he was so very afraid. Could he come over and see me?

He was there within the hour, grey with fear. If this was what the entertainment business had done to him he would have been far better off among the small tame animals and little cage birds that were the passion of his life. It might well come to that, I thought, when I heard his story. He had a bad cough; for the past ten days he had been coughing up blood. The doctor, whom his manager had called in, had told him there was nothing at all to worry about. But he was worried, he couldn't sleep because he was so worried. I had seemed so sympathetic to him, did I think there was anything else he should do, like seeing another doctor, perhaps?

I certainly did. But I remembered, from the time I had incurred the wrath of the Beatles' road manager, by offering one of the priceless quartet a powerful cold-cure tablet, just before a performance, how very tough and scathing managers of pop stars can be if anyone threatens to interfere in the mildest way, with their hot property. On the other hand, coughing up blood seemed a serious matter. It aroused all the protective or maternal or better instincts which, professionally speaking, I hardly knew I possessed. While the pop star drank a much-needed glass of hot milk, I phoned his manager — and got an enormous flea in my ear, for the trouble, plus a reluctant promise that, when the show ended in three week's time, he would let his protégé be checked over by any Harley Street chest specialist he cared to name. This seemed to cheer the singer up enormously and, armed with the name of a London chest specialist I knew, he returned to his fans and his responsibilities. Ten years later, he was still top of the bill.

From pop stars, I jolted my mind back to the unmentionable lion and the authoress who was definitely in need of a drink, a little stronger than a glass of hot milk. A neat whisky restored her to such an extent that she remembered that it was long past the time when she should have taken her tranquillising tablet. With shaking fingers she fumbled in her capacious handbag and from its depths extracted a tiny, ornate pill-box. Carefully, she studied its contents, selected one of its rainbow-coloured assortment, gulped it down, snapped the box shut and, returning it to its handbag, leaned back with a deep sigh and closed her eyes, as if waiting for the pill to take effect.

Suddenly, the blue eyes shot open and she sat bolt upright.

"Did you see what colour tablet I took?" she demanded. I thought it was a blue one.

"Oh GOD!" she moaned, cradling her arms across her chest and rocking backwards and forwards in distress, "I think I've taken a sleeping pill."

Half-an-hour later it was fairly obvious that she had.

I ordered black coffee and kept up an inconsequential, non-stop demanding sort of conversation. She stayed awake and, gradually, it looked as if everything might be going to be all right; perhaps even more than all right, for she was becoming calm and relaxed, and just a little dreamy, which for any authoress was more than permissible.

It was time for transmission: in the studio, waiting for the red light to come on to indicate we were on the air, she leaned back in her chair with perfect composure. The camera men adjusted focus, the seconds passed, as we waited under the hot arc lights. The red light flashed, the linkman started his introduction to our item and I glanced across to make sure that she was listening. Horrified, I saw that her head had fallen forward on her chest and she was snoring, gently.

I leant forward and shook her, roughly. Her eyes blinked open, she stared round, dazedly and at that moment, she was on the air. It would take a miracle to jerk her back to reality to give a performance; any sort of performance . . . There was just one hope: I went in blandly and unkindly:

"In your book you wrote about Magic, your favourite lion . . . " The blue eyes stared, coldly, but it had registered and I persisted,

"Tell me about him," I said, playing for time, "tell me how you first met and everything that happened to him."

She sighed and was shocked into wakefulness; but not too shocked:

"It all happened such a long time ago . . . " she began and told the story of Magic, with not the trace of a tear.

7

Degrees of Involvement

IT is almost impossible to work on a story, for any length of time, investigating it in depth, for a few weeks, for a radio or a television feature, and not become personally involved. Take, for instance, an assignment to discover the more unusual items which it was possible to hire: they ranged from a pair of sugar tongs to an elephant and, between these extremes, for the appropriate financial outlay, there was no problem about becoming the temporary owner of such impressive possessions as a replica of the Crown Jewels, valued at nearly twenty thousand pounds; a friendly camel, docile enough to be ridden down Oxford Street in the evening rush hour; or a breath-taking azurine, grey mink coat which swept the floor and was guaranteed to be an eye-catcher at any London premiere, in justification of the hiring cost of £40 an outing.

But it was the simplicity of hiring an escort, that really caught my imagination: I felt that, in the cause of professional authenticity, this was the one item that justified the closest personal scrutiny. And so it happened, that for an initial outlay of £10, I became the owner for one night, in a manner of speaking, of Peter Moncrieff. (Not that this was his real name, nor even the nom-de-plume he usually worked under.) But at less than one-fifth of the cost of a camel, he seemed a pretty good bargain, particularly as he would be put down to expenses.

He was on the books of a West End agency who had their offices on the second floor, over a Piccadilly tea-shop. The rooms inspired confidence; they consisted of a soothingly-decorated, executive type of suite presided over by an ex-colonel type of Managing Director who I took completely into my confidence and explained just why I was so keen to hire his most "typical" male escort. Whether or not he was entirely convinced that I was motivated purely in the cause of professional duty, remained rather doubtful. He kept emphasising, almost too knowingly, that most ladies were invariably rather shy and full of excuses, in the initial stages of their first transaction of this kind. However, in all his years in the game, there had never been one lady client he had failed to put at her ease.

His clients were of all ages and both sexes, in about equal proportions. He had many success stories to tell like the one about the young man of nineteen who wrote to enquire if he could hire a mother. He was a youngster from a very humble background, but he had done well in his job and his employers were considering earmarking him for spectacular promotion. However, before reaching their final decision, they thought it might be useful to know a little more about his background and meet his parents.

This was the last thing the young man wanted to happen. For various reasons, he doubted whether either of his parents would be anything but a handicap in furthering the image he had been at such pains to create. So, using the very initiative which had put him in line for promotion, he decided to take no chances: he would hire a suitable substitute; "A lady in her early forties . . . Not too smart . . . quiet and pleasant-looking," was how he set out his requirements. The agency supplied the very person.

Make-believe mother and son got slightly acquainted in the taxi on their way to the vital interview but not nearly thoroughly enough for the escort to be able to cope with all the questions fired at her by the three directors of the firm employing her newly-acquired son.

She was an actress and she decided, this time, the only possible approach to the part was to "play it for real" and portray, even exaggerate, the nervousness she was most certainly experiencing: accordingly, whenever she did not know the right answer to the questions, she twisted her handkerchief in knots, bowed her head in embarrassment and mumbled.

"I'm afraid I just don't seem to remember what happened . . . " or "I really don't know what to say . . . ," seemingly, quite confused and out of her depth by it all; which, of course, she certainly was.

" . . . The mother's a lady, all right," was the undoubted verdict, " . . . But it's lucky the son hasn't inherited her lack of confidence . . . Probably takes after the father!" Anyhow, they gave him the benefit of the doubt, according to the fulsome letter of thanks he sent to the agency, announcing he had got his promotion. Compared with such machinations, my requirements were modest in the extreme.

Armed with two complimentary theatre tickets, for the premiere of a new play, I met Peter Moncrieff, as arranged, in the foyer of the theatre. As in all the worst romantic novels, he wore a red rose in his lapel and carried a furled umbrella.

The theatre had been a touch of inspiration: it seemed the least agonising way of spending the evening with a stranger who might turn out to be a complete bore. It would also keep the expenses down, for in addition to the initial hiring fee, I was, of course, responsible for the cost of the evening, including food. I fervently hoped the gentleman was not ravenously hungry and in the habit of regarding such an outing as first and foremost, a gigantic meal ticket. If so, he was in for a big disappointment.

As it turned out, the pleasant-looking middle-aged man, standing by the box office, was neither hungry, nor a bore. He obviously saw nothing unusual in a blind date with a dark-haired lady in a black velvet trouser-suit whose husband had been, unexpectedly, called abroad on business and who needed a male escort to take her to the theatre. It seemed a pretty lame excuse for dating a strange man, but it was the best I could manage and I assumed, he must have heard many lamer ones! In the course of the evening, it transpired that he certainly had.

During the first interval, I learned that my companion was, by profession, an actor. He also had a university degree in Experimental Psychology. The escort business gave him an opportunity to practice both skills. When he was "resting" as an actor, in between parts, he usually managed to find a daytime teaching job. Then, in the evenings, it was pleasant, once or twice a week, to go out on the town, all expenses paid, plus a fiver in his pocket afterwards.

He had done escort work, on and off, for about five years and it was, definitely, the opportunity to use his acting talents that most appealed to him.

"It's great, sometimes," he confided, with genuine enthusiasm. "You're acting a part but, at the same time you're doing it for real. And — and this is the really exciting bit — for once, you're not cut off from your audience, away up on the stage. You're right with them, surrounded by them, say in a room full of well-dressed very intelligent people. And they mustn't even know you're acting . . . "

He gave me a recent example: he had acted the part of an army officer, a Major, at a wedding reception attended by many army officers and their wives. He was escorting the wife of a Major who had been posted overseas, just before the wedding. It was held in Cambridge. His companion hardly knew anyone there, but rather than go alone, or worse still, stay at home and miss the chance to show off the extravagant new outfit she had bought especially for the occasion, she decided to complete the picture and set it off with an appropriate husband-substitute. No wonder Peter Moncrieff had accepted my equally lame excuse for hiring an escort, at its face value.

There were many similar stories. He was such an excellent conversationalist, thanks perhaps to the degree in psychology, that I relented and invited him to onion soup and spaghetti-bolognaise at a bistro, near the theatre. I overcame any problems about the bill by passing him a folded five pound note, with the coffee. He paid for our meal, tipped the waitress, scooped up the change and, pocketing five shillings for our taxi, pushed the remaining silver back to me with no sign of embarrassment.

At this stage, in an evening that had passed so quickly and pleasantly, I had an irresistible desire to take him into my confidence and redeem myself in his estimation by confessing that, far from being an oversensitive female who needed a man around so much that she was prepared to pay for the privilege, I too had embarked on the evening as just a "professional" engagement. Moreover, I was longing to get out my note-book and pencil and jot down some of his stories.

I was afraid I would never remember some of the details of his tales of escorting wives who'd discovered their husbands were taking out the secretary or who thought the best way of curing their husband's seven or fourteen or twenty-one-year itch was to retaliate in kind, but avoid genuine involvement by hiring a rival to parade in front of the erring husband, to rouse his jealousy. This remedy, Peter assured me, often worked. I made a mental note!

He told me of the time he went to a Deb ball, masquerading as a French Count, complete with dark glasses and a broken English accent. He was partnering a debutante whose girl friend was having an affair with some minor nobility and who wanted to go one better. Deb dances, it seemed, were thick with escorts. It was their busy season with non-stop requests for their services from anxious mothers whose one fear was that their ugly-duckling daughters might be left as wallflowers.

I had certainly had my money's worth and had plenty of material for my purpose. It was time to end the unexpectedly-enjoyable evening, a 'bonus', I congratulated myself, for doing a job so diligently! Once again, I longed to confide in Peter, but, after he had spoken so frankly, it seemed rather a mean trick to admit that I had, in a way, tricked him.

At my hotel, he handed me out of the taxi and paid off the driver. He said he would walk home. We went into the hotel and shook hands, rather formally, while he thanked me for a pleasant evening. For the first time since we'd met I felt embarrassed. But there was worse to come: out of the corner of my eye, I saw my husband, back earlier than I had expected, not from the fictitious trip abroad, but from a genuine long-standing all-male business dinner.

I had taken him into my confidence about my all-in-the-course-of-duty expedition and he was sitting at a corner table, having a drink and waiting for me to come home. I waved to him, nonchalantly, but he was not to be put off.

It was an hour later when I retired to bed and left them to it, talking away like a couple of school-boys, until the small hours.

* * *

Hiring an escort is something that, in real life, under certain circumstances, I could just bring myself to do. But wearing secondhand clothes — never. That as far as I was concerned, was a retrograde step I would never even consider. I would prefer to "make do and mend", queue for sale bargains or even learn to make my own clothes before subjecting my flesh to the indignity of an unknown woman's garments, with their musty smell, or unfamiliar odour of a strange dry cleaners.

Weeks of research on the subject, for a programme called "Secondhand Rose", only confirmed my deep-seated resistance to the market in this particular commodity although, in the course of investigating, I acquired a healthy respect for those who cashed in on the business side. They included earnest gentlewoman who, from the kindness of their hearts, ran discreet charity shops selling cast-off clothing which they elevated to the title of "nearly new" and the "thrift shops" where anything, however shabby, could be sold at a price.

When it came to making a good living from the business there was no-one to touch the gentleman "Wardrobe Dealer" who, in response to a post-card or telephone call, arrived at the seller's home, exactly at a pre-arranged time, in his opulent car. Speed was the essence of his visit. With a flourish, such as Sir Walter Raleigh must have used when he flung down his cloak before Queen Elizabeth I, he spread a clean dust sheet on the bedroom floor, or wherever the cast-offs were displayed for his pleasure, made a cursory examination of each one, dismissed the suggested price with a hollow laugh and, peeling off pound notes for about half the expected total from an impressive wad of money from his back pocket, dropped all his purchases into the dust sheet, bundled it up, flung it over his shoulder and was away, without giving the seller time to have second thoughts.

There was not a moment to spare, it seemed, on this country-wide clean-up of discards from extravagant fashion — conscious housewives, for ever seeking space for their new purchases in already over-crowded wardrobes. For some reason however, the gentleman who fulfilled this service, invariably rejected at least one of the garments on offer, leaving it drooping dejectedly on its hanger, a token perhaps of the fine sense of discrimination of this connoisseur in the business.

Ironically however, the very cream of the secondhand clothes market had, I found, fallen, almost by accident, into the perfectly-manicured hands of two beautiful society sisters who, for more than a quarter of a century, had reigned as undisputed queens of international hand-me-down haute couture.

Ever since the war, one or other of them had presided over their exclusive little Kensington shop, where some four

271

thousand model garments from the best fashion houses in Europe hung from rails, all round the walls.

June Hamilton, the blonde and beautiful elder sister, had trained as a model, but during the war, ended up working as a "steel roller" in a Sheffield iron foundry. Roma, the young, dark one, was still at school. After the war, they both went home to their parents' luxurious London flat and planned a winter sports holiday at St Moritz, while they decided what they should do with the small shop in Sloane Street which their mother had offered to take for them.

Just three weeks before they were due to leave for Switzerland, their home was burgled and all their smart, new holiday clothes, representing their entire ration of clothing coupons, were among the things stolen. In the scramble to replace them, they discovered that at dress agencies they could buy secondhand clothes for only half the number of clothing coupons required for new ones. It would be quite a joke, they thought, to try and run a dress business like this, in their little shop, much easier than a florists which meant getting up at 5 a.m. each day to buy fresh flowers.

On opening day, a pre-war, black silk tulle ball-gown of June's filled the whole of their tiny window. Within an hour it had sold for £15. They were on their way. By the time clothing coupons were abolished, they had worked out a well-tried formula and established an exclusive clientele, stretching all over the country. Like a very secret society, its members were referred to only by a number.

The system worked like this: Client "A" would bring four model gowns into the shop and leave them. June, or Roma, checked through the files and contacted client "B" who was roughly the same size as "A", and with similar tastes, to see if she was interested in buying the garments, which may originally have cost between fifty and three hundred pounds each. The sale price varied between one-fifth and one-seventh of the original price. Client "A" would get no money until her clothes were sold, whereupon the sister took between twenty-five and thirty per cent of the sale price.

The real secret of their success was

their insistence on accepting only "top label" clothes, in immaculate condition and usually, not more than one year old. Today, they boasted, they turn away eight garments for every one they accept, can tell the difference between a French and an English made hook-and-eye and an American and an Italian manufactured zipp-fastener. In any case, clients who tried to fool them by substituting exclusive continental labels for those of ready-to-wear British firms, usually came unstuck at the seams, for "finishing off", they told me, varies from country to country. Moreover, it appears there's much more to a simple thing like sewing on a dress label than meets the eye.

Clients, if their names could be disclosed, were straight from the society columns of the top newspapers: they included a couple of European princesses, the wives of cabinet ministers and ambassadors, some not too distant Royal relations and a host of Mayoresses and politician's ladies who, faced with a non-stop round of public appearances, found the place a godsend. Besides these, and less in the public eye, there was a steady stream of debutantes and their mothers. There were also the wives of officers in Her Majesty's Armed Forces; they stocked up their wardrobes, whenever they were home on leave, with good quality clothes which they could not normally have afforded and which would certainly help to preserve a picture of British elegance, in far-flung places.

Surprisingly, there were many clients who both bought and sold; anxious for a quick change of costume at bargain prices and with enough "savoir faire", if accosted by a friend saying,

"My dear, you're wearing my dress!" to reply, coolly:

"Oh, so you go to Valentino too. How naughty of him to make so many repeats!"

The dedicated sisters, whose flourishing business, started "just for fun" grew beyond all belief, did all they could to prevent such confrontations. If they suspected a purchaser moved in the same circle as the original owner of the dress she had just bought, they made discreet enquiries about where she intended to wear it. Fortunately, they managed to prevent a deserted wife and the co-respondent in her divorce suit, from buying each other's clothes, but were unashamed at being instrumental in the photographs in *The Tatler*, two years running, showing the same outfit at Ascot, on two different owners.

Despite their system to preserve anonymity among their clients, I found the atmosphere in the tiny shop more like that of a pleasant little club than the secret mecca of countless under-cover financial transactions. No less than eight assistants were on hand, to help and advise; a well-known actress was flitting about in bra and panties, trying on one extravagant outfit after another and appealing, to anyone and everyone, for advice on its suitability. The wife of one of the country's most senior statesmen, looking faded and weary in old-fashioned knee-length bloomers was being fitted with a heavily-beaded dinner gown.

The only touch of discretion was a liveried chauffeur who arrived bearing a pile of dress-boxes, and stood, twiddling his moustache with embarrassment, as he caught a glimpse of the near-nude actress, while he waited for the contents of the boxes to be examined and receipts made out for the ones that were accepted.

There was nothing in the least musty-smelling or sordid about this set-up! On the contrary, the tiny shop was more like an Aladdin's cave: I fingered exquisite ball gowns of soft chiffon with jewel-encrusted bodices, whispering black taffetas and glowing brocades whose labels showed they were the pick of the world's collections.

And then, I saw IT — a simple understatement of woven gold with a collar of coral and jade stones; Christian Dior, Paris; just the dress I'd have chosen, could I have afforded it. And then, I realised, I could afford it. There was no earthly reason why it couldn't be mine — except that I didn't wear secondhand clothes. Still, there was no harm in just trying it on, to see how I looked in it.

It was no hardship to slip into this silk-lined luxury: it conveyed no smell of any dry-cleaners. Just the merest intoxicating suggestion of good times that had gone before. Or were they still to come?

My deep-seated old-fashioned scruples disappeared in two seconds flat. This was a solution to gracious living. Just a small alteration round the waist and in less than half-an-hour it was mine and we were on our way.

Two months later, I slid into it again, on the night of the Regimental Ball. This should confound my husband. I would keep my evening cloak on and not show it to him until we arrived. It confounded him all right.

"What's that queer smell?" he said, when we were in the taxi.

"What smell?" I asked, innocently, "I don't notice anything."

He sniffed determinedly.

"Your perfume," he pronounced triumphantly. "You've changed your perfume. It's most odd. It just doesn't suit you. What's wrong with the stuff you always wear? It's much nicer."

So much for the intoxicating suggestion of good times! With the warmth of the taxi, an unmistakable smell of "Joy", the most expensive and persistent perfume in the world, was slowly and persistently emanating from my gorgeous bargain. It seemed advisable not to try and explain it away. Husbands can be conservative creatures.

★ ★ ★

Judging at baby shows and beauty competitions is, without doubt, one of the most unpleasant by-products of public life. Nearly all the babies who appear in the line-up are beautiful or cute or jolly-looking and to have to express a preference for three or four of them and then select one miniature supremo, is the saddest and most fatuous exercise I am ever invited to perform.

The only consolation is that the poor mites have no idea what is going on. But the mothers do. I suspect that I have made more enemies at Saturday afternoon garden fetes than in all the battles, official and otherwise, I have ever been involved in.

There is a strong case, I suspect, for abolishing these invidious contests for such innocent and tender victims. However sad it may be for the defeated babies, the outcome for the winners may prove far more disastrous. Once they have tasted success, some ambitious mothers aspire to bigger and better things and I recall a certain "Miss Baby Soap" competition where I was re-introduced to a hideous ringleted four-year-old whose blushing mother assured me that I was the person responsible for her daughter entering it. It seemed I had encouraged her by awarding her first prize in the village baby show, three years previously.

I wracked by brains to recall how I could possibly have made such a mistake and decided it must have been her red hair that caught my eye: it probably looked a good deal more appealing in its primary, fluffy stage than coiled into fearsome ringlets. Anyhow, I felt I had a good deal to answer for!

Once competitors are old enough to have the vote, however, it becomes a rather different matter, with judging organised on a systematic basis. As a judge, I frequently find myself in complete disagreement with the men adjudicators on most of the detailed merits of the entries. However, when all the marks are added up, with a little juggling and some generous compromise, the best girl for the job usually emerges winner, even if she does happen to have the thickest ankles.

On the rarest of occasions, thick ankles or no, there is an unbelievable sense of relief when one of the competitors possesses that indefinable magic called "Star Quality" which transcends all attempts to give marks for individual points like "hair" or "deportment".

The little, dark girl in the area finals for the National Queen of Industry had "Star Quality" all right, and very little else. She had obviously set her hair herself; her deportment was only fair and, at sixteen-and-a-half years old, her poise was negligible. Moreover, when she walked, her white slip showed a good half-an-inch below the hem of her dress. Yet, in comparison, the other eleven entries, with their carefully-lacquered hair-styles and practised smiles, seemed unexciting replicas of each other.

Before the parade, we talked to each of the girl's in turn. I spoke to the little, dark one last of all; she had a soft, husky voice and a bewitching smile. If she could iron out her accent she would be the stuff of which film stars, rather than stage actresses are made, I thought.

Surprisingly, the male judges were inclined to agree. Not that this was borne out in their marking for when the cards were totalled up, she was third in the list. Something would need to be done:

"That dark kid's the only one who's got anything about her. Pity she's so young . . . " conceded the head of a chain of fashion stores who happened to be visiting the area and had been persuaded to be one of the judges.

"I agree," said the university lecturer on the panel, adding that he doubted whether, whoever won the heat, would get far in the final of the contest, in London in six weeks time.

By mutual accord, we looked at our mark sheets again and, made a few small adjustments. The next time, the little dark girl came first.

No-one was more surprised than she, when the result was announced. But she carried it off well, with an unexpected dignity and she smiled, bewitchingly, when she shook hands with each of the judges in turn, thanking us most graciously. You can tell a good deal from a handshake!

During the rest of the evening, I did not seem to be able to get her out of my mind. Neither, it seemed, could the fashion tycoon. Over coffee, he re-opened the subject:

"I hope she gets a decent dress to wear for the final," he ruminated.

"And a proper hair-do," I added.

He sipped his coffee, thoughtfully.

"Tell you what," he said, eventually, "if I arrange for one of our shops to give her a dress, as an extra prize, will you supervise the hair-do?"

"Yes," I said, "but that won't be enough."

"Enough for what?"

"To stand a chance in the Final."

"Could she?"

"She just might," I said, "a slim one. If she were determined enough. But it would be a hard six weeks, learning what it takes."

He thought about it.

"If I foot the bill, will you help her?" he said.

"No thanks," I said. "Why should I? In any case I'm far too busy for any Pygmalion act."

Out of the corner of my eye, I could see her, flushed and excited, holding court, across the room. Her hair infuriated me.

"No reason at all, why you should, except for the fun of it," said the tycoon, "I dare you to have a go."

"Dare me to do what? A Rex Harrison? Not on your life!"

"Put it this way," he said, and I remembered his reputation as a gambler, "I'll give £25 to your favourite charity if you get her groomed to come in the first four in the final."

"Make it the first six," I said. "She's not really tall enough."

"Done," he said, and we shook hands.

Her name was Victoria and she was a machinist in a local shoe factory. She liked her job. Her friends had dared her to go in for the competition — just for the fun of it! So she too, couldn't resist a dare! I learned about it on the way to the hairdressers, our first priority. We went to my own hairdresser who, when

I explained the position, volunteered to take over this part of the responsibility for free. I felt he too, was longing to get his hands on that luxurious, ungroomed dark mop. I, thankfully, left her to his ministrations.

Two hours later, with her hair swinging, pertly, just above her shoulders, she looked fantastic. I took her to lunch, but she was so excited, she could hardly eat a thing. She had never dreamt her prize would include deportment and elocution lessons, but she admitted it was just as well because she felt awfully nervous at the thought of going to London for the final.

"No need to worry," I said. "You can learn a lot in six weeks."

She did too: in her lunch hours and in the evenings. Once a week, we met, to discuss her progress. For some reason, she never queried my part in the affair.

"You're taking an awful lot of trouble with me," she said once. "Do you always do this after a Beauty Contest?"

"Not always," I said, and we left it at that.

There was the day when she asked me

if I would help her to choose the dress:

"We'll find the best in the shop," I said. We did too. Deep pink chiffon, spotted with crimson; disconcertingly demure with its full skirt gathered into a tiny waist. Satin shoes were dyed to the exact colour of the crimson sash and she found a lipstick, just the same shade. There was to be no glimpse of petticoat showing next time she paraded before the judges.

In the tremendous London ball-room, she stepped out onto the huge dance floor, smaller, younger and daintier than the others. She walked well now, head high, black hair swinging. She looked like a confident young Romany in an extravagant red gown, billowing in soft folds from her tiny waist. She was proud, yet somehow vulnerable. The applause, after the first stunned silence, was tremendous.

"I'd never have believed it," murmured the fashion tycoon, reaching for his cheque book: she was placed fourth. She was a connoisseur's choice, too subtle for a Beauty Queen.

That evening, I met her parents, for

the first time. After the judging, she brought them over to our table, for introductions — the gruff-voiced Irish labourer, uncomfortable in his blue suit and the plump Eurasian he had married when he was a sergeant in India and she, no doubt was a slim dusky maiden. So this was how Victoria came by her olive skin and shining, black hair!

"We would like to thank you," she said, with Victoria's smile. "She's a good girl. We're glad she's had her chance."

It had all been well timed. There was a nice young man at the ball; he worked in a bank. Possibly, he was also a bit of a connoisseur, in a manner of speaking. Anyhow, he and Victoria were married three months later and, as far as I know, they lived happily ever after. Which all goes to show, beauty contests, once a girl's reached the age of consent, aren't necessarily bad things!

8

With Advancing Years

AGE, for a television performer, is a serious business, it seems: the Soho theatrical agent who suggested that it was time he took my rather chequered career in hand, was adamant about it.

"How old are you?" was the greeting he shot at me, after I had climbed up two flights of narrow, rather rickety stairs, to his cramped, untidy little office, for our first meeting. Only the framed photographs of current celebrities, adorning the walls, all dedicated to him, according to their signed inscriptions, with the utmost gratitude of the sitters, suggested the climb might, just possibly, be worthwhile.

He contemplated me, speculatively, pulling on his over-sized cigar, a living caricature of his profession, and waited for my reply. I was ready for him: I stared him back, straight in the eye and sliced five years off my age.

"Never say that again," he roared and for one shattering moment I thought I had underestimated him and he had seen through my modest little deception. It was a painful moment, but before I had time to wilt under its full implication, I realised, with a delicious thrill, I had underrated myself.

"For one thing," he continued, through clouds of cigar smoke, "you don't look your age." I could have kissed his dear, ugly face.

"Secondly, once a woman's past thirty, her age is no asset, so it's best to ignore it altogether."

"Suits me," I agreed, "but not everyone I meet seems to think that way. If I'm asked, point blank, how old I am, I can hardly pretend to have forgotten."

He gave me a fair impersonation of a sophisticated middle-aged starlet avoiding an issue, or rather of a male impersonator giving an impression of a middle-aged starlet:

"Just say, quite nonchalantly, 'How old do I look?' That's all that matters," he advised waving the cigar nonchalantly.

He developed his case: I was indeed one of the fortunate ones, and not only because I had been discovered by him, just in the nick of time; I was equally blessed because my face had no JOWELS. By the look of it, it might never have any JOWELS. The whole thing was just a matter of bone formation. That was the first thing he looked for. And providing I kept the other two big give-aways of female age, the elbows and neck, nicely under-cover, it was his opinion that I could go on working for both of us on the television screen, for quite a few years to come.

I pulled my scarf up a little higher at my throat, thanked him for his advice and said I would think about it. The next day I bought half-a-dozen long-sleeved, polo-necked sweaters and decided to embark on a new ageless existence — all on my own!

It was rather ironical therefore that the question of age cropped up, officially and unavoidably, just one week later. It arose because I was to fly in a new type of power-glider to do a radio report about the machine. With timely consideration, my employers decided it was a good moment to take out an insurance policy, on my account, just in case of an accident while I was working for them. Accordingly, they supplied a long and rather involved form for me to fill up, with all the relevant personal information. The third question on the form was "AGE?"

With the agent's recent admonishment in mind, I deliberately deducted five years. After all, they were hardly likely to go to such lengths as asking to see my birth certificate. Half-way down the page however, they did seem to be checking up on this one, with the trick question "Date of birth?" I was ready for it. Once again, I neatly deducted the five years.

Three days later the form was returned to me by the Office Manager. "They won't insure you" he said, with a bland grin, "until you explain just how it comes about that there is ten years' discrepancy between your date of birth and your age." Alas! mathematics never were one of my strong points.

Of course, in comparison with many, very old and usually very active, senior citizens I meet, I am still entitled to consider myself a mere chicken. Certainly, I felt that way compared to the ninety-six year old East Anglian chemist, with a prodigious memory who, over the years, provided me with a steady source of income.

We met for the first time, when he was acclaimed the oldest dispensing chemist in the country:

"Don't all these new-fangled drugs confuse you a bit?" I asked the chivalrous old gentleman, in a black coat and striped trousers, who looked as if he had stepped out of another age.

"The drugs are all right," he replied, without a moment's hesitation. "It's all these blessed cosmetics that get me down."

It was not long before he became a regular broadcaster, chiefly because of his ability to recall the smallest detail about events that happened long ago, well before the turn of the century. Hardly a month went by but that, armed with a portable tape-recorder, I drove to the little village where he lived, to interview him about the origins of some current topic of controversy. He was an historic broadcaster, in every sense.

He was also lonely, having been a widower for many years and there were no signs of his children around. It was his loneliness, he told me, that after he sold his own chemist's shop, when he was just on eighty, prompted him to answer advertisements in the trade journal and go anywhere in the country doing locum work. But when he was ninety years old, he found travelling round the country and working in strange surroundings a little tiring and so he decided to settle down. Thereupon he bought another chemist's shop, a very small one, in his own village.

It was there I interviewed him for the very last time. I had telephoned to say I was coming to talk to him about his memories of the first Bank Holiday, a public holiday that was introduced when he was a boy. Did he remember it? Did he just.

"You mean Lubbock's Law? Of course I remember," he had said on the 'phone, without a moment's hesitation.

"I was a boy at the time; about ten years old, I suppose. We all went to the park ... " and he was off with his reminiscences. I told him to hold it! I'd be down with my tape-recorder.

I arrived at his shop just before closing time. On a sudden impulse I had taken a small present, as a token of my admiration for the way he could always be relied on to turn up trumps: it was a large, blue, ornamental match-box, an appropriate gift for such a confirmed pipe-smoker, but suddenly, as he unwrapped it, I realised it could hardly have been a more unfortunate choice, for it was painted with a gold laurel wreath, a decoration which for anyone of ninety-six must surely look more like a funeral wreath than a symbol of Roman greatness.

He thanked me, gravely, but with a rather rueful look, as if he had just been reminded that time was running out. Or was that my own over-vivid imagination? Anyhow, I wished I had never bought it and suddenly all I wanted, was to get the interview over and done with as soon as possible.

The assistant left. He locked the door after her and pulled down the blind to show the shop was closed. Meanwhile, I arranged two chairs, close together, in front of the counter with the tape-recorder on a stool nearby. We sat down, I turned on the recorder and asked him a couple of questions to try it for level, whereupon it was obvious that the shop, with its glass-fronted cupboards, glass counters and carpet-less floor offered a pretty poor acoustic. To mitigate this, I turned down the volume level on the recorder and pulled our two chairs as closely as possible together. I turned on the recorder again and posed the first question. Simultaneously, I felt a hand steal across and very gently and quite deliberately, grip my left knee.

Time was running out indeed! My immediate reaction was to push the hand away. Then, half in admiration and half in sympathy, I changed my mind. Perhaps mine had been the first move, with an unsolicited, ill-chosen gift and this was his reaction. Or perhaps, at ninety-six years old, he felt he was entitled to a bit of harmless fun. If so, good for him! In any case, he was a lonely old man. As it turned out, he only had a few more weeks to live so I never saw him again. But I have never, for a moment, regretted doing that one recording with an old man's hand resting, comfortably and companionably, on my knee.

★ ★ ★

There was another day and another old gentleman, when the hand-on-knee interviewing situation was completely reversed, this time for a television film. The subject was a grand old Fenlander who had written his first book *Tales from the Fens* and had it published, when he was over seventy. And if that wasn't an achievement in itself, he only started to write his book after he had become stone-deaf and completely bed-ridden with a paralysis of the legs. On the face of it, he was likely to be the easiest subject to interview, particularly as he had never even seen a television set.

Jack Barrett, a gentle giant of a man, had been born with a caul over his head, a membrane which sailors look upon as a charm against drowning and which the Romans considered the equivalent of "being born with a silver spoon in one's mouth." In the Fens, it was supposed to endow a child with the gift of the gab which, in Jack Barrett's case, translated as pencil and paper, is just what it had done, although it had only become apparent, as the *Sunday Telegraph*, neatly put it, "at the eleventh hour".

That was when I arrived at the tiny stone cottage in the grounds of one of the big houses where, until the paralysis set in, he had worked as a gardener, until long past the age of retirement. Then, bedridden, he had passed the days, remembering the stories he had heard in his youth, when he worked as a "crow-scarer" for 3d. a day and had written them all down in longhand.

They were excellent stories, tales of legend and flood and unrest in the Fens, from before the turn of the century, all laced with a peculiar grim humour. He remembered hearing them, he explained in the introduction to his book, because he had left school at eleven years old, when his brain was quite uncluttered with facts and figures.

It was as a young lad that he met the great American story-teller Mark Twain. The writer had been staying in Cambridge, after a nervous breakdown, and was advised by friends to move to the Fens, to complete his recuperation at the Ship Inn at Brandon Creek. This was just near Jack Barrett's home and his best friend's father was the inn-keeper. Fortunately for the young story-teller-to-be, he was prepared to turn a blind eye to the two young lads sitting in the corner on Saturday nights, listening spell-bound as the old men told the tales, handed down from their fore-fathers. Mark Twain too, relished the story-telling which continued until either the beer or the money ran out for there was no question of calling "Time gentlemen, please" in a place where no policeman would care to venture out, after dark. Mark Twain made a great impression on all the children by having an inexhaustible supply of sweets to hand out to them, so they followed him everywhere. Nevertheless, it was as a teller of stories that he was best remembered by the young Jack Barrett.

Some sixty years later, his brain was still as clear and lively as a boy's and his eyes danced merrily, although the only possible way to communicate with him was to write everything down on a large note-pad he kept by the bedside.

His huge bed occupied most of the tiny sitting room. From its depths, he presided over his world, a silent monarch whose every wish and need was anticipated and interpreted by his round, bustling little wife who, conveniently enough, was a trained nurse. But as soon as she had ushered me into the room and settled me in the chair at the head of his bed, he waved her, imperiously, from the room, giving me a conspiratorial wink.

It was perhaps as well, for there was certainly not an inch of room to spare, not even for the cameraman. He had to set his tripod up outside in the garden and focus the camera through a conveniently-situated window.

Meanwhile, I worked out an elaborate filming procedure which I wrote down in detail on the bedside note-pad. The loud chuckles of glee from the bed, indicating the occupant both understood and approved, brought his wife back into the room again, to be dismissed unceremoniously, with another wave.

The procedure I outlined to him was this: I printed the questions in huge script on three large cards and propped them up against the foot of his bed, so that he could see them but so that they were just out of range of the camera. I then posed each question in order, while he, supposedly staring into space as I talked, read it off the card and was ready with his reply as soon as he saw my lips stop moving.

After a little practice he announced he was ready to have a go but I still wasn't satisfied. By this time, he almost knew the questions off pat and there was a certain artificiality about his timing and the way he jumped in with his answer, almost anticipating the question. The solution, as I suggested it on his pad, produced even louder roars of approval and the return, and instant dismissal, of his ever-watchful spouse. This, he indicated to me, was not intended for her eyes: nor, as far as I was concerned, for anyone else's. That indeed, was the whole purpose of the carefully-contrived operation.

From my bedside position, I could just manage to lean towards him sufficiently, holding the microphone in one hand, to conceal the fact that my other arm was under the bedclothes, making contact with his leg. Whenever I posed a question, he was to wait, before starting his reply, until he felt my nip on his leg, as the signal to begin talking.

The result, when we saw the film's rushes, was a sensation. This great character of a man, just head and shoulders, fairly leapt from the screen, eyes alight, the moment I posed my first question.

"You didn't have much time for reading, when you were a boy," I asked "but you did have the chance to meet that great story-teller Mark Twain?"

He listened, alert and eager with a reflective gleam in his eye. There was a pregnant pause, which transfixed the viewers, while he apparently revelled in his memories of meeting the great writer. He was revelling all right, in the unfamiliar sensation of feeling a strange woman's hand under the bedclothes.

It proved a most satisfactory operation and there was to be an even more satisfactory sequel: Jack Barrett wrote two other successful books, but even more important, quite soon after my visit, after being bed-ridden for eleven years, he, almost inexplicably, regained the use of his legs. I couldn't of course, claim to have had a hand in it. But I like to think I perhaps offered just the mildest stimulation!

* * *

After interviewing a seventy year old author who was stone deaf, it seemed only a logical challenge to try and record a radio interview with a ninety-five year old one who was both deaf and blind. She was Miss Dorothy Thompson who finished writing her first book when she was ninety-three years old.

It was the story of her father, a Suffolk parson, and his life and times in the

Victorian/Edwardian era. Dorothy was his eighth child, but not until she was eighty-four years of age and starting to go blind did she commence writing his biography, tracing the family history back five generations, to her great, great, great grandfather the Rev. George Lauder, great grandson of Sir Robert Lauder of Lauder and Bass, who was obliged to flee from Scotland to England in 1689 when William III forbade the use of the Prayer-book. He did the journey on foot, carrying his youngest daughter and his enormous Bible, which was in two parts. Dorothy Thompson apparently inherited from him both longevity and strength of purpose.

As an author, she certainly needed both these qualities, for when, at long last, she succeeded in finishing her real-life story with its personalities ranging from distinguished, ancestral clergymen to Suffolk fishermen and including Elizabeth Garrett Anderson, Britain's first lady doctor, her well-meaning but misguided friends, with their strict Victorian upbringing, were shocked that she had mentioned people by name and insisted that she destroy the manuscript. But, with Scottish caution, before doing so, she rewrote her story, editing the original and retaining just a few of the names of real people, towns and villages. She then destroyed her first incriminating manuscript.

Her friends were still not satisfied. They felt that even the few names in this second version were quite enough to identify some of the characters. So Dorothy Thompson, bowing to public opinion, embarked on a third version of her book, when she was eighty-seven years old. This time, with anonymity and propriety fully preserved, a friend volunteered to show the book to a publisher.

After the publishers had read the first seven chapters of the book, they were puzzled because they seemed to be reading the story all over again. The second time round however, it was told in a much livelier and more colourful way, with the characters really coming to life. They were, in fact, reading part of the second manuscript which had somehow become mixed up with the final version. This, they decided immediately, was the manuscript they wanted to publish, rather than the final version which, with the removal of all traces of real people had lost much of its vitality.

But not Dorothy Thompson. At ninety-three years old and still receptive to criticism, she made one proviso; that if after all, this was what the public really wanted, she would sit down and write them an even better story. To her sceptical publisher's amazement, over the next few months, this was exactly what she did. Just before her ninety-fifth birthday, Dorothy Thompson, authoress extraordinary, held the published version of *Sophia's Son*, the story of a Suffolk parson, in her hands, although by this time she had become too blind to see it.

That was when I went to visit her, in her neat little house in a quiet road in suburban Hertfordshire. She lived entirely alone, fiercely independent, surrounded by pictures and ornaments and Victorian bric-a-brac, souvenirs of her younger days. She had a friend, living nearby, who came in every day to light her fire; that was all the help she needed. I had written to say I was coming and the friend was there. Through finger language, she communicated my arrival to the frail, white-haired old lady, in the arm-chair by the window, wearing a black dress and a lacey shawl, which matched her soft hair. A heavily-jewelled cross hung from a thin gold chain round her neck.

There was no need for her to voice her delight at my visit; her gentle, deeply-lined face glowed her pleasure and her sightless blue eyes smiled. There was so much I wanted to ask her, but it was a slow business because I could only talk through her friend's fingers.

Dorothy Thompson completely understood the mechanics involved in making such a recording. To ask a question, I would turn on the tape-recorder, pose the question and turn the machine off again while the friend relayed the question to Miss Thompson, in finger-language. There was a pause, while she considered her answer, quietly and deliberately and then, just as we had arranged, she would nod her head, as a signal that she was ready for me to switch on the recorder, wait a second or two and then, with the utmost composure, as if she had been doing this all her life, reply to the question, with great enthusiasm and obvious enjoyment. For this short time, her fine brain was able to communicate and converse again, regardless of physical limitations. I felt a sadness at the inevitability of its re-imprisonment, as for an hour or more, Dorothy Thompson answered my questions about her own life and experiences, in her clear, precise voice that was so symbolic of her writing.

In her shaky, almost illegible hand-writing she autographed my copy of her book and thanked me for coming. I left her to her fire and her memories and went home to edit the tapes, joining my questions up to her answers and condensing our conversation down to the conventional length for a broadcast. Of course, Dorothy Thompson never heard her voice telling her own story over the air. But very soon afterwards, she did hear that her book had gone into its second edition, and had also been produced in braille and as a talking book.

Where longevity was concerned, Mrs Ada Roe of Lowestoft, who lived to be nearly one-hundred-and-twelve years old, was certainly the 'Daddy' — or rather 'Mummy' — of them all, and, during the last years of her long and active life, I established a very happy relationship with her.

It was a working relationship: we met, for the first time, when she was already something of a national celebrity. I had turned up, with a portable tape-recorder, to interview her for a radio programme. She lived in a little back-street dairy, with her name emblazoned over the top of the door, just for sentiment's sake I thought, pushing open the door.

The bell clanged and a tiny old lady, her hair screwed up in a little bun on the top of her head, looked up at me from behind the counter:

"Good-morning," she said.

"Good-morning," I replied and, feeling my way, "can I have a pint of milk, please?" She handed me a bottle and the change for my money.

"Does old Mrs Roe live here?" I asked.

"I am Mrs Roe."

"I mean the Mrs Roe who's a-hundred-and-six."

"It's my birthday today," she said. "Look at all my cards and flowers. Isn't everybody kind?"

It seemed hardly possible: no spectacles, sprightly; good hearing. How could this perky little soul have been born in Islington when Disraeli was an up-and-coming politician and when Charles Dickens was putting the finishing touches to his *Little Dorrit*? If this was the lady I had come to see I'd heard that when she was fourteen years old she had worked as a machinist with a firm making underclothing and had earned two-and-six pence a week for nine-hour working days.

It was her all right. She told me that the first time she had visited Lowestoft, she was on her honeymoon and she had fallen in love with the place. Her husband was always ailing and, at the turn of the century, she persuaded him to move there because she believed the bracing sea air would do him good. It did. He was healthier than when he lived in London, but in 1910 he died, leaving her with three daughters and a dairy to run which meant pushing a hand-cart round the streets, delivering milk, which she continued to do until she was seventy years of age.

While she was telling me this, an elderly woman shuffled into the shop:

"Come on, Mother," she said, "I'll look after the shop now. Your tea's waiting."

"My eldest daughter," explained Mrs Roe, and I thought I detected a twinkle in the blue eyes.

Over the next six years, I saw those eyes twinkle many times. Every year, she became more famous; at one-hundred-and-eight, at the Royal Norfolk Show, she was introduced to the Queen Mother; on her one-hundred-and-tenth birthday, she made the *Guinness Book of Records* and a West End hairdresser insisted on coming from London to give her a special hair-do. He was photographed, surveying his handiwork, in most of the national newspapers. Meanwhile,

Mrs Roe was feted and dined and photographed opening an Old People's Home; she took it all in her stride and loved every moment. It made a nice change from pushing a milk cart round the streets.

Every birthday, after she was one-hundred-and-eight, she received a crate of grapes from Covent Garden and a world-wide authority on longevity booked a room at a local hotel to ensure he would be the first on hand to wish her "Many Happy Returns of the Day". But every year, I managed to beat him, and the rest of her admiring public, to it.

Every year, at the beginning of February, I would turn up at the dairy about a week before the birthday, with a small present, not for Mrs Roe, but for her very much over-shadowed eldest daughter. A bowl of flowers, a box of chocolates or a small plant, as a token acknowledgement that in a few days' time, it was she who would be Mistress of Ceremonies, in supreme charge of all the arrangements at her mother's birthday. A cup of tea and a chat with them both and I'd be away, with a cheery wave from Mrs Roe:

"See you next week," she'd call; "mind you come early before all those newspaper men!"

I made sure of that!

Every year, while the gentlemen of the press gathered impatiently outside the front door, waiting for admission, I and the television crew would be inside, cables coiled around the tiny sitting-room, filming the birthday interview. And, every year, I found it harder to think of a suitable birthday present to give her.

On the one-hundred-and-tenth birthday, I took her a bottle of sherry.

"Pour out a glass for all of them, dear," she said to her watch-dog of a daughter.

"Pour it out for them yourself," her daughter countermanded. This then, was the stuff of longevity.

It grew harder too, to vary the birthday interview; I had asked all the obvious questions so many times. The last time of all, when she was the oldest woman in Britain, it seemed better to cut out the interview and simply film her receiving her present.

She had deteriorated a little over the previous year and had taken to wearing steel-rimmed spectacles, at times, but not, of course, in front of the camera. On my pre-birthday visit, she had grumbled, for the first time ever, because, during the winter, she had submitted to being seen by a doctor and "had never felt right since."

But on the actual birthday, she was suddenly as cheerful and on form as I ever remembered:

"What have you brought me?" she kept asking, but I parried with her, until the cameras were ready to register her surprise when she opened the parcel.

Her present was a soft blue, mohair stole. As the camera turned, I put it round her shoulders.

"It's lovely," she said, stroking it sensuously. She threw back her head and the blue eyes twinkled:

"Does it suit me?" she said. "Do I look nice?"

"You look lovely," I said, and I meant it. "I want to wish you Very Many Happy Returns of the Day." And I took her hand.

"Your hand's cold," she said, "perhaps it's you who should have the stole! Anyway," and she gestured towards the fire, "warm yourself before you go home: We won't charge you any more . . . "

Mrs Roe died just one month before her next birthday. The last film was taken out of the library to be shown again, on the night of her death, all over the country. I was to introduce it, telling her story over another short film made up from some taken during her earlier years. But just as the red light flashed in the studio, indicating I was on the air "live", there was a hitch because of a fault in the machine running the film. Instead of the expected picture of Mrs Roe on the monitor screen, I saw a shot of myself in the studio, waiting to begin reading the commentary. Simultaneously, I heard the producer's voice through my ear-piece shouting to me to "waffle, just waffle 'till we sort it out."

I stared at the camera. This was a performer's nightmare. Desperately and deliberately I collected my thoughts and made the following pronouncement to the waiting nation:

"I have known Mrs Ada Roe of Lowestoft, for a long time." I paused, and waited for inspiration. It came:

"I knew her when she was a-hundred-and-six . . . I knew her when she was a-hundred-and-seven . . . " I was in my stride " . . . and one-hundred-and-eight" By "a-hundred-and-nine", when I was almost beginning to enjoy myself, I heard through the ear-piece the film was just coming up. Rushing through the last two years, I timed it nicely and cued in, neatly, if unconventionally:

"Do I look nice?" she asked once again from the screen, snuggling into the mohair stole and preening like a schoolgirl. And the blue eyes seemed to twinkle.

I sighed with relief. After the anguish of waiting for her to appear, at that moment, she looked to me, nicer than ever!

★ ★ ★

Every impressive elderly citizen has their own recipe for successful longevity: the actress, Dame Sybil Thorndike, for instance, confided to me, when she was nearly ninety, that she owned her marvellous memory to the fact that every morning of her life, before getting up, she memorised twelve lines of Greek verse. On the other hand, Horace Bull of Cambridgeshire, who at ninety-three was awarded the national title of "Veteran Angler Extraordinary", by an angling magazine attributed much of his staying-power to his tattered sixty-year old shooting jacket.

It was a double-skinned, greenish affair, rendered all the more waterproof because, over the years it had become impregnated with the grease and salt of a thousand shooting expeditions over the bleak Fens and fishing trips, out in the North Sea. It had been repaired at most of the seams, with thick black thread and, more recently, as the fabric itself gave way, with layers of once-pink sticking plaster, wherever it required reinforcement. It was rather reminiscent of the one-time East Anglian Bishop who, in his old age, stuck stamp-paper over a crack in his spectacles, rather than get a new pair.

Wearing this jacket and with a thick

wool muffler bridging the gap between it and his checked deer-stalker, its owner was impenetrable to any amount of British weather. At over ninety, during a shooting expedition, he had been stranded alone, all night on the marshes, during a snow storm and had kept warm by holding a dead goose he had just shot, firmly between his knees. (No doubt the shooting jacket protected his upper regions!) At first light, he found his way to a marshman's cottage, dumped the goose, had some breakfast and, without a wink of sleep, went back to the marshes after duck and snipe, for the rest of the day. This tough and tenacious character had offered to give me my first lesson in sea angling.

I was not a complete novice at sea fishing, but before then I had only fished from a moving boat: it was during years of summer holidays at Sheringham that I learned the fun of spinning for mackerel, trailing three or four lines behind a motor boat, chugging along less than half a mile off shore and, after half-an-hour, getting back in time for breakfast with more than enough fish for everyone in the boat.

If there is anything more delicious for breakfast than mackerel, fried in butter and eaten within an hour of being caught, I've yet to taste it.

At the other end of those long, summer days at Sheringham sometimes when the tide and wind were just right, there were stealthy night-time excursions to net the local salmon. These salmon-trout or sea-trout are virtually indistinguishable in flavour and appearance from the river variety and, I'm told, that where the Scottish lochs join the sea, the question as to whether a fish is a salmon or a sea-trout provides a fine point of argument for keen anglers.

That's as may-be but certainly no true angler would condone the method I learned for catching the local delicacies, 'though it had an excitement all its own and, as my companions eased the rowing boat down the slip-way, over the crunching pebbles and into an almost motionless sea, at dead of night, I felt I was setting sail with pirates, not with fishermen.

I clambered into the boat and sat in the stern while the men rowed, until the twinkling lights of Sheringham receded into the dark and were blotted out by the towering cliffs. The oars were muffled and, almost silently, the boat glided along the coast for about two miles and turned inshore, at a small bay. A few yards from where the single line of surf edged the beach the men lifted their oars and remained motionless, listening intently for perhaps ten minutes. Then, almost like a pre-arranged signal for our rendezvous, came a faint splash from across the bay, and then another, louder one.

A third splash — nearer and much more gentle, was our anchor going overboard, carrying one end of the hundred-and-twenty yard net; we then swung the boat across the bay in a wide semi-circle, playing the net out behind us like a giant spider's wed, suspended in the water from a row of bobbing corks.

There was no longer any need for stealth: with long canes we beat and threshed the water as we crossed and recrossed the bay, inside the barrier made by the net, hoping to scare any fish caught there and drive them into our web. One enthusiast climbed out of the boat and like some fantastic merman, sparkling with phosphorescence, he waded waist deep, sweeping the water with an oar, into swirling pools before him.

"There he goes — a beauty!" he shouted as a flurry of silver foam splashed against one part of the net. He climbed back into the boat and, while two oarsmen steadied it on course, I helped to haul the dripping net back into the boat, armfuls at a time until at last our quarry came with it: a gleaming six-pounder, still struggling for its freedom. A few yards further along the net was another, smaller one.

By the time the dawn broke, we had spread the net more than a dozen times — always in a slightly different stretch of water and had caught about fourteen large salmon trout.

The fishermen reckoned I was lucky to them, even though I had not been born with a caul over my head! Years later, on the day of my angling lesson with Horace Bull, the fish were also biting!

On a grey, March morning the skipper of our little open boat *Cheerio*, which at first light, had chugged out of Lowestoft harbour, dropped anchor, near the Corton Sands, three miles along the coast. There was an uncomfortable swell on the water and, while Mr Bull was not looking, I hastily swallowed a sea-sick pill. So did the television crew who were balanced with their equipment across the stern of the boat, to record the proceedings. They were both keen fishermen and had volunteered for the job.

Horace Bull ignored them completely, once the fish started to bite and we began pulling in fine two and three pound codlings, just as fast as we could rebait our hooks. It could not have been stage-managed better: soon the buckets were brimming with fish from the five lines, for even the camera crew had wedged a couple of rods over the stern. There was a fraught moment when the boat lurched, while they were reeling in a catch and only a frantic leap on the part of the boatman, Bob Williams, prevented several thousand pounds worth of equipment from pitching overboard.

Horace Bull hardly seemed to notice,

or if he had, he decided to ignore it, just as he turned a blind eye to his discomforted friend who had called for him before dawn that day, to drive him the sixty or so miles to Lowestoft and who, for most of the time, was neatly and apologetically sick over the side of the boat, pills and all.

Such human frailty went apparently unnoticed by the "fen tiger", crouched over his rod, fishing in the lee of the wind, behind the wheelhouse super-structure, in his favourite corner of the boat. He emerged occasionally to show me how to put a particularly succulent worm on my hook or help me, very chivalrously, to disengage a stubborn catch from my line. Periodically, the cameras whirred into action to record the proceedings.

Some six hours and several hundred cod later, my fingers numb with cold, they turned for one last take, and my final interview.

"This must be a marvellous sport, in summer?" I prompted my venerable tutor, with agonised conviction, for the film's benefit. He reeled in his line. He had fished enough for one day.

"Yes," he agreed, with unexpected fervour, "I can't wait for the summer," and he eyed me speculatively.

He was, suddenly out of character, acknowledging to the world that he was a fair-weather fisherman. It just didn't ring true.

"Why do you so much prefer fishing in summer?" I persisted. He grinned, like a twelve year old naughty schoolboy.

"Because of the girls in their 'Hot Pants'," he cracked back, ending the interview with the sort of comment that more than justified my half-day spent tossing about in the grey North Sea in an open boat.

Three months later, a parcel was delivered at the office: inside was a small pair of scarlet 'Hot Pants' and a note from Horace Bull:

"I won these in the raffle at our village garden fete," he wrote: "they reminded me of our good day's fishing. I hope you will accept this little gift from an old man, in the spirit in which it is sent. How about a return trip?"

This then, is the stuff of a ninety-four year old "fen tiger."

Of all the old people, it was a fellow journalist, Elizabeth Craig, the doyenne of all cookery writers, who gave me, not only some excellent food recipes, which I tried out immediately, but the formula I should, one day, most like to be able to try out, her personal formula for a successful old age.

On her ninetieth birthday, I went to record a radio interview with her in her Norfolk home that was once a monk's sanctuary, half of which was destroyed, by fire, during the Great Plague. Now, a haven of panelled walls and great open fire-places and old, polished furniture, it's crammed with the treasures acquired during a life-time spent in many of the capitals of Europe, writing of the pleasures and passions of food, drink, places and people and also, as the wife of Arthur Mann, the American foreign correspondent, whom she married in 1919.

She opened the door to me, wearing a pair of well-cut, maroon slacks, a matching polo-neck sweater, (shades of my would-be agent). She had rather reluctantly, agreed to take time off from writing her thirty-first book and meeting the deadlines on three magazine articles, to talk to me. When I arrived however, there was no sense of urgency; she was obviously prepared to talk for hours, about anything and everything under the sun, while her husband, who in his green eye-shield, looked as if he'd strayed from his newspaper office, produced non-stop cups of delicious coffee that, eventually, were displaced by glasses of fine sherry. He confessed that he had given up writing, long ago, even 'though he was ten years younger than his wife. Sometime, between the coffee and the sherry, he pottered off to do the shopping.

The simplest of the food recipes, and therefore the one I liked best, was for an easy party sweet that didn't take a minute to prepare. It entailed placing one or two rounds of tinned pineapple in the bottom of a flat sundae glass, covering with a thick layer of grated milk chocolate, and topping with whipped cream, flavoured with rum.

The other recipe, for such an active

and successful old age and being wooed by editors and publishers at ninety years old, required much longer preparation. She summed it up, in the warm, Scottish accent which years of international living only seemed to have exaggerated.

"I love my work," she said. "I couldn't do anything else. I can never sit still. I can curl up like a cat and sleep at any hour of the day and night. I sleep in the trains. But when I'm awake, I'm just thrilled with living. Fancy sitting down like a cabbage, when you get your pension, as some people do, just watching the television and waiting to die. Life is, for me, far too thrilling for that."

We talked about writing.

"What's the title of your book?" she asked me. I told her.

"I'll give you a better title," she said. "'Don't Switch Off'". That about summed it all up!

9

Not Quite the Last Word

STRAIGHT reporting, interviewing, commentating, call it what you will, the best of journalism, for me, is two-fold. It's a profession that pushes me into doing things that, normally, I would never even have considered and, now and again there's the unexpected touch of magic which crops up in a story, providing the same sense of satisfaction a musician must feel when he composes a perfect phrase, or a painter, when he steps back from his canvas and says "It's like!"

As for the unsought experiences: in the normal course of events, I doubt if I would have walked along an underground tunnel, a hundred and fifty feet below the streets of Norwich, to meet the "soft-ground miners" building a new sewer; cheerful Irish navvies who were delighted to down tools and chat with a "dame" in their white, warm world of compressed air, where the chalk dust mists up in damp clouds and where the only vegetation is the pink fungi which flourishes abundantly in the tropical temperature.

I would certainly never have been persuaded to fly in the back seat of an American trainer jet fighter, have ridden the foot-plate of an express steam locomotive, or sailed in the Yarmouth lifeboat, *The Louise Stephens*. Nor would I have realised how perilous it felt to ride on top of a stage-coach, in the good old days: if I was shaken about on a commemorative ride on a straight ten miles stretch of the A.11 from Norwich to Wymondham, how much worse it must have been for travellers in the days of rough roads and highwaymen.

On the commemorative ride, staged by a firm as a publicity stunt for their two hundreth anniversary, we too had our highwayman who galloped out of a side road and held us to ransom for charity. The firm, who had supplied magnificent period costumes for all the coach party had even remembered to provide a "bag of gold", evidence of that meticulous attention to detail which no doubt had contributed to their commercial success over two centuries. Their thoroughness also extended to "suitable sustenance" before the return journey, at *The Old George and Green Dragon Inn* in the shape of a banquet of boar's head, suckling pig, pumpkin pie, syllabubs and port-soaked stilton which demonstrated, rather conclusively, that the olden-day traveller must have had a stronger digestion than a modern journalist.

Where food is concerned, if it were not for my job, nothing would have induced me to sample the dubious delights of plastic manufactured meat, dandelion leaves or common limpets, prised from the rocks by a young free-food fanatic who had just written a book about Nature's largesse.

It was only in the course of duty that I came to have my hand-writing read by Jeanne Heal, journalist turned scientific graphologist, when I invited her during an interview on a television programme, to demonstrate her skill by analysing the handwriting of an anonymous person called "Sara Harrison". It was a neat disguise, I thought, to hide behind my second name and my maiden name. But there was no disguising the penetrating science of graphology.

"This is the handwriting of an outstandingly dedicated career girl," Jeanne announced, although she had not the slightest idea who Sara Harrison was. "She is living under severe strain, which is entirely self-imposed because she forces herself to subjugate all her normal and domestic feelings to the tremendous demands she is making on her mind and her imagination . . . Her job will unerringly take precedence over her private life . . . " I had heard enough; I admitted I was Sara Harrison and hastily changed the line of questioning, fervently hoping my husband was not watching the interview. On the way home, to salve my conscience, I bought a knitting pattern for a man's golf sweater, in two-ply wool. Somehow, as someone whose handwriting showed "the tenacity of Roosevelt", I vowed I would manage to finish it.

As for the unexpected touch of magic; I found it in listening to the old-fashioned butter maker describing, when she was ninety years old, how, as a young girl, on the day of the County Show, she got up at three o'clock in the morning to carve her freshly-churned butter into the shapes of flowers and birds and fluffy, golden ducklings: "Everything was golden," she said, her dim eyes dreaming back into the past, " . . . pure gold. And there was the sun, rising all pink and gold, and I felt just like a queen on Show days, in my freshly-starched pinafore . . . "

Then there was the day I launched a ship; precipitating, by just touching a button, the champagne to break over her bows and her inevitable moment of birth, so that she stirred and moved irrevocably down the slipway, meeting head on, with a soft sigh, her destiny in the grey waters of the North Sea.

I remember a very old man who had been blind from birth and who spent all his spare time doing his garden. He was very fortunate, he said, because there was no need for him to stop gardening and go indoors when it grew dark. In his slow, countrified speech he explained how, just by touch, he could tell the difference between a red rose and a white one.

I can hear the telephone ringing, as if it were yesterday, with an unexpected call from a mother whose twelve year old son had run away from home. He had been gone for ten months after disappearing without trace and she had almost given up hope of ever seeing him again. The 'phone call was to say he had just walked into the house. He had decided to go home after seeing me tell his story on a television programme about "Missing People".

Magic moments, all of them, but if it weren't for my job, I might never have had a chance to share them. I would certainly have had no part in the real-life story of a little Chinese girl called Pik Yuk, whose name in English means "Translucent Jade".

Pik Yuk was nearly four years old when we met, to make a little film about the first chapter of her life. This began, according to her birth certificate, when she was "found abandoned beside the Roman Catholic Cathedral, Caine Road, Hong Kong, on or about 1st October, 1958."

According to the *Daily Express*, who along with most other national newspapers, splashed the story of her arrival in England across its front page, "The pale lemon-coloured baby girl had been found, wrapped up in a newspaper on the Cathedral steps." She was headline news when she was carried off the plane on her arrival at London Airport from Singapore, by the wealthy, Irish-born tobacco magnate and his elegant wife, who planned to adopt her and bring her up in the utmost luxury and who were taking her to their beautiful country home in Cambridgeshire, to be brought up with their own three children.

About two months later, I went to their home, a grey Georgian house set among four acres of beautifully-tended grounds with neat lawns and fruit trees and a stream, to do a television story about how Pik Yuk was settling down there; I was solemnly introduced to the tiny, exquisite, ivory doll with a mop of short, straight, black hair that swung and shone, animated by her every movement. She had enormous jet-black almond-shaped eyes and she was a beauty in anybody's language.

She welcomed me with her carefully-rehearsed "How do you do?" She was a little shy, but she was already perfectly at home in this house of near-oriental splendour, filled with jade carvings, Thai silks and rugs and paintings and other treasures acquired, no doubt, on frequent business trips to the East by this world director of a tobacco empire and his wife. It was almost as if Mr and Mrs O'Neil-Dunne had, without knowing it at the time, designed their home especially to receive Pik Yuk. There was even a Chinese cook called Hop Yee and a pair of Pekinese dogs for her to play with.

Pik Yuk romped with them over the lawns for our camera, gay and spontaneous and enchanting. She rode her tricycle and played on the swing, just as we asked, with none of the usual coaxing and patience invariably required before young children and animals will be persuaded to perform. She showed no inhibitions or self-consciousness and, although she could hardly have understood a word we said, she twinkled and laughed and posed and showed off a little, like a born actress.

When we eventually returned to the house I took off my sheepskin coat and put it on the hall seat. Immediately Pik Yuk seized on it, threw her arms round it and hugging it to her, buried her nose in it, sniffing vigorously, like an excited puppy. She always behaved like this, it seemed, and at the last dinner party, while her parents' guests were downstairs, she had been found in the bedroom, sniffing at all the visitors' fur coats.

There was no explanation for it, they said, just as there was none for the way, night after night, she screamed out in terror with mysterious nightmares that she could not describe in her limited English. And by day, like a magpie, she collected keys and trinkets and bright, inconsequential objects and hid them away, under her pillow.

Her mother told me about it, over coffee. She described how Pik Yuk, after being found on the Cathedral steps, had been cared for by the Canossian nuns, together with two thousand other Chinese babies, in one of their orphanages, nestling high up on one of the steep hills of Hong Kong Island. It was on a casual visit there that she and her husband saw the sallow, shabbily-dressed toddler who clung, whimperingly, to the Mother Superior's habit and decided they would like to adopt her.

The adoption formalities were long and involved, because Pik Yuk had already been made a ward of court. For two years the only tangible promise of her new life was the steady supply of vitamin tablets and gift parcels of clothes and toys that arrived for her from England.

The first of many legal formalities was to appoint as her guardian the Director General of Social Welfare in the Colony of Hong Kong. This guardianship was then transferred to the Bishop of Northampton in England. Once that had been accomplished, a little Chinese waif, born with only a one-in-four chance of ever learning to read and write and with the prospect of being so hungry that she would, one day, be glad to eat from the bark of a tree, was on her way to a new home, within sight of the spires of

Cambridge University. In her suitcase, on a piece of blue paper, was a list of essential Chinese words, written down by the nuns who had looked after her.

There was to be a good deal more paper-work before Pik Yuk could be legally adopted and registered at Somerset House, in the splendid names of "Dominica Marie". All the family made the most valiant attempts to use the new name. But it was no good, the youngest Miss O'Neil-Dunne would remain "Pik Yuk" for the rest of her life.

She played on the hearth-rug, periodically hiding her face in the fur of one of the dogs, while her mother told me about these things and explained why, with three children of their own, she and her husband had decided to adopt a Chinese baby? It had, by no means, been a sudden decision: there had been complications at the birth of the last child, so that she could never have another child of her own.

Child-welfare had always been one of her prime concerns. As for her husband: all their married life he had been so totally involved with business and so completely committed that he had hardly been able to take any active part in the upbringing of his own three children. He would soon be reaching the time of retirement and Pik Yuk could give him the chance to play a father's role in her education, interests and hobbies. She might even help him to learn how to be a little young again.

But why adopt a Chinese child? The need of these children, she said, was often so much greater. There were hundreds of them, proud descendants of an elegant and ancient nation, living in the most pitiful poverty. Their culture was so much older than ours. They had invented printing while our ancestors were still living in caves.

They welcomed publicity for Pik Yuk, not because of what they had done, but because the International Children's Welfare Society thought it might encourage other people to follow suit and consider adopting some of these children.

It was easy while she was a baby, but when she grew up, what would happen if either of their two sons fell in love with her and wanted to marry her? Cecilia O'Neil-Dunne felt that, at any rate, she would have had plenty of say in the way her daughter-in-law was brought up!

This eventually was broached sooner than anyone could have expected when Pik Yuk was just five years old, in fact, and Timothy, her favourite brother and the nearest to her in age, was ten. Solemnly, he asked their father for her hand in marriage but he was told that, because they were brother and sister, it would be necessary to write to Pope John for permission.

"Write! Why can't you telephone?" demanded the impatient suitor.

"What's your hurry?" asked his father.

"Well, Daddy, she's behind the door, waiting for an answer."

There must have been many occasions, since then, when Pik Yuk has waited for an answer but never once, to everyone's surprise has she shown curiosity about her natural parents or her native background. But there have been many times when a father of four children has had the novel experience of being invited to wrack his brains to cope, not with world-wide financial problems, but with far more insoluble ones, fired at him, without warning, right in his own home:

"Daddy, why can't the Pope make mistakes?"

"Why do people say dreams go by opposites?"

"If we can't bear to kill and eat our own chickens, why do we kill and eat other people's?"

The next time I met Pik Yuk she was fourteen years old wearing jeans, her black hair swinging provocatively. She was unexpectedly tall and rather shy and very beautiful. I learned that she was clever for her age and musical and a bit of a tom-boy. She told me that, when she grew up, she wanted to be a P.E. instructor. Perhaps she will be, if she stays with this ambition for she can certainly, I understand, run and jump and swim faster and further than any girl of her own age, in the school, and most boys too. Just for the record, she doesn't really like watching television because she usually knows how the stories will end; chocolates make her sick, but not nougat and she loves horse-riding, classical music and her brother Tim.

This book began with a quotation from an Eastern prophet. It ends also with a writing from the Orient; part of a composition by Pik Yuk, a Chinese teenager, growing up in Cambridgeshire.

One day perhaps, Pik Yuk will write her own story, telling it much more fully and vividly than I have done. But telling stories like hers, and encouraging people to relate their own is, for me, the most satisfying job I know. And if Pik Yuk, by seeing herself in print, is encouraged to persevere with her own literary efforts, for me to have had a share in this will more than atone, I feel, for quite a fair-sized chunk of neglected housework.

Appendix

Spring by Pik Yuk

SPRING is between black winter and red summer. Spring in England is a new life for me. Spring is more light and less darkness, Mummy spring-cleaning and Daddy becoming busy in the garden. Chiffon, my dog, is in season. Leo howls and scratches the door — such a nuisance! All the pets are moulting, hairs everywhere and the Hoover bag gets filled up more quickly. I am kept busy fetching and carrying and helping to turn the linen in the cupboards.

Spring is swallows and starlings coming back and when William's peacocks howl "Aow! Aow!" as though they were hurt; but I know they're not suffering because it's their Spring call.

Spring is daffodils and daffodown-dillies. Yellow sunshine comes close to the ground. When I look higher, to the branches of the trees, the yellow turns to pink and white and then to green. The frost comes but the flowers don't seem to mind. Nor do I because it's getting warmer outside and the days are getting longer.

Spring is all the lovely bulbs springing from the ground. I like the smell of hyacinths best, a blue, white, red and pink perfume. It is cherry and almond blossom time. I prefer to stick their stiff branches higgledy-piggledy into the flower bowl because it's so easy and looks quite nice and lasts longer. Spring is a budding time, flowers everywhere, as lovely as dreams.

Spring is much beauty. My goldfish stir and swim faster. Time to start feeding them again. Spring is trees turning green, then greener and all of a sudden, all GREEN. Yesterday the fields were brown, now they look greenish and pinkish at sunset.

Winter is dead; church bells ring; Lent is over. No more purple in church. Now it's Easter, hot cross buns and Easter eggs. I paint funny faces on them, but for Mummy I write in colour: 'I love you'. Sometimes it gets warm and sometimes cold, but more warm than cold — the other way round to Autumn. I no longer hurry home from school in the dark. There's more light — true light, not electric light. Everyone seems to be in their gardens. No more overcoats, no more woolies, no more gloves. They've all gone to the dry-cleaners.

In the middle of Spring, showers turn to drizzle and fierce winds stop. Daddy and Joe cut the grass and I breathe the smell of new lawn-cuts. Spring is when we start swimming in school and play rounders. Boys give up football for cricket. All the garden furniture comes out from winter storage and we scrub them and put them on the patio. Everyone helps to get the pool ready, especially me, because I love swimming. It's nicer swimming in our home pool, the water is much warmer than at school.

Spring is the Boat Race on T.V. First it's Cambridge, then Jarlath's Oxford. We cheer them both and they both win: nobody comes last — just first and second. Daddy switches to horse-racing every Saturday, while I help Mummy with the flowers and lawn edges or we wash and brush the pets.

As Spring gets warmer it's harder to study. Soon there are so many exams. I am busy, inside and out, because it's Spring. All the pets and birds and chickens help me to keep busy, because they're also busy. Spring brings honey bees, wild bees and bumble bees. I read that in Spring, all bumble bees are queens because in the wintertime, the male bumble bees freeze to death. Spring is caterpillars turning to moths and butterflies. Some are pretty, some eat our woolies.

Spring is ladybirds waking and hiding their golden and red speckles in warm places. I'm careful not to squash or tread on them because they eat the greenflies which eat our rosebuds. Earthworms are busy on the lawn. Tim put one in my bed and scared me stiff. Funny to be frightened of an earthworm between the sheets and not when it's outside. It creeps slowly, yet it's hard to catch it to give to my goldfish who will eat it if it is cut up.

Spring springs everything to life. It is the season of marriage and birth.

The newspapers have wedding pictures of smiling couples. This is Spring. I don't notice it when Spring departs though, because Summer follows next. And Summer is first "springer", then "springest" Spring.

THE WILDERNESS WALK
Sheila Bishop

Stifling unpleasant memories of a misbegotten romance in Cleave with Lord Francis Aubrey, Lavinia goes on holiday there with her sister. The two women are thrust into a romantic intrigue involving none other than Lord Francis.

THE RELUCTANT GUEST
Rosalind Brett

Ann Calvert went to spend a month on a South African farm with Theo Borland and his sister. They both proved to be different from her first idea of them, and there was Storr Peterson — the most disturbing man she had ever met.

ONE ENCHANTED SUMMER
Anne Tedlock Brooks

A tale of mystery and romance and a girl who found both during one enchanted summer.

CLOUD OVER MALVERTON
Nancy Buckingham

Dulcie soon realises that something is seriously wrong at Malverton, and when violence strikes she is horrified to find herself under suspicion of murder.

AFTER THOUGHTS
Max Bygraves

The Cockney entertainer tells stories of his East End childhood, of his RAF days, and his post-war showbusiness successes and friendships with fellow comedians.

MOONLIGHT
AND MARCH ROSES
D. Y. Cameron

Lynn's search to trace a missing girl takes her to Spain, where she meets Clive Hendon. While untangling the situation, she untangles her emotions and decides on her own future.

NURSE ALICE IN LOVE
Theresa Charles

Accepting the post of nurse to little Fernie Sherrod, Alice Everton could not guess at the romance, suspense and danger which lay ahead at the Sherrod's isolated estate.

POIROT INVESTIGATES
Agatha Christie

Two things bind these eleven stories together — the brilliance and uncanny skill of the diminutive Belgian detective, and the stupidity of his Watson-like partner, Captain Hastings.

LET LOOSE THE TIGERS
Josephine Cox

Queenie promised to find the long-lost son of the frail, elderly murderess, Hannah Jason. But her enquiries threatened to unlock the cage where crucial secrets had long been held captive.

THE TWILIGHT MAN
Frank Gruber

Jim Rand lives alone in the California desert awaiting death. Into his hermit existence comes a teenage girl who blows both his past and his brief future wide open.

DOG IN THE DARK
Gerald Hammond

Jim Cunningham breeds and trains gun dogs, and his antagonism towards the devotees of show spaniels earns him many enemies. So when one of them is found murdered, the police are on his doorstep within hours.

THE RED KNIGHT
Geoffrey Moxon

When he finds himself a pawn on the chessboard of international espionage with his family in constant danger, Guy Trent becomes embroiled in moves and countermoves which may mean life or death for Western scientists.

TIGER TIGER
Frank Ryan

A young man involved in drugs is found murdered. This is the first event which will draw Detective Inspector Sandy Woodings into a whirlpool of murder and deceit.

CAROLINE MINUSCULE
Andrew Taylor

Caroline Minuscule, a medieval script, is the first clue to the whereabouts of a cache of diamonds. The search becomes a deadly kind of fairy story in which several murders have an other-worldly quality.

LONG CHAIN OF DEATH
Sarah Wolf

During the Second World War four American teenagers from the same town join the Army together. Forty-two years later, the son of one of the soldiers realises that someone is systematically wiping out the families of the four men.

THE LISTERDALE MYSTERY
Agatha Christie

Twelve short stories ranging from the light-hearted to the macabre, diverse mysteries ingeniously and plausibly contrived and convincingly unravelled.

TO BE LOVED
Lynne Collins

Andrew married the woman he had always loved despite the knowledge that Sarah married him for reasons of her own. So much heartache could have been avoided if only he had known how vital it was to be loved.

ACCUSED NURSE
Jane Converse

Paula found herself accused of a crime which could cost her her job, her nurse's reputation, and even the man she loved, unless the truth came to light.

CHATEAU OF FLOWERS
Margaret Rome

Alain, Comte de Treville needed a wife to look after him, and Fleur went into marriage on a business basis only, hoping that eventually he would come to trust and care for her.

CRISS-CROSS
Alan Scholefield

As her ex-husband had succeeded in kidnapping their young daughter once, Jane was determined to take her safely back to England. But all too soon Jane is caught up in a new web of intrigue.

DEAD BY MORNING
Dorothy Simpson

Leo Martindale's body was discovered outside the gates of his ancestral home. Is it, as Inspector Thanet begins to suspect, murder?

A GREAT DELIVERANCE
Elizabeth George

Into the web of old houses and secrets of Keldale Valley comes Scotland Yard Inspector Thomas Lynley and his assistant to solve a particularly savage murder.

'E' IS FOR EVIDENCE
Sue Grafton

Kinsey Millhone was bogged down on a warehouse fire claim. It came as something of a shock when she was accused of being on the take. She'd been set up. Now she had a new client — herself.

A FAMILY OUTING IN AFRICA
Charles Hampton and Janie Hampton

A tale of a young family's journey through Central Africa by bus, train, river boat, lorry, wooden bicycle and foot.

THE PLEASURES OF AGE
Robert Morley

The author, British stage and screen star, now eighty, is enjoying the pleasures of age. He has drawn on his experiences to write this witty, entertaining and informative book.

THE VINEGAR SEED
Maureen Peters

The first book in a trilogy which follows the exploits of two sisters who leave Ireland in 1861 to seek their fortune in England.

A VERY PAROCHIAL MURDER
John Wainwright

A mugging in the genteel seaside town turned to murder when the victim died. Then the body of a young tearaway is washed ashore and Detective Inspector Lyle is determined that a second killing will not go unpunished.

DEATH ON A
HOT SUMMER NIGHT
Anne Infante

Micky Douglas is either accident-prone or someone is trying to kill him. He finds himself caught in a desperate race to save his ex-wife and others from a ruthless gang.

HOLD DOWN A SHADOW
Geoffrey Jenkins

Maluti Rider, with the help of four of the world's most wanted men, is determined to destroy the Katse Dam and release a killer flood.

THAT NICE MISS SMITH
Nigel Morland

A reconstruction and reassessment of the trial in 1857 of Madeleine Smith, who was acquitted by a verdict of Not Proven of poisoning her lover, Emile L'Angelier.